New Humanism

New Humanism

BY

M. N. ROY

GYAN

Published by

Gyan Publishing House
5, Ansari Road
Daryaganj, New Delhi-110002
Phone: 011-47034999, 9811692060
E-mail: books@gyanbooks.com

Distribution Network
gyanbooks.com
India, USA, Canada, UK, Australia

ISBN: 978-93-6280-594-2 (PB)
First Published, 1939

2nd Impression 2024

Printed at: Gyan Press, Delhi.

NEW HUMANISM
Author: M. N. ROY

New Humanism

A Manifesto

By

M. N. ROY

1990

CONTENTS

PREFACE

The Conference of the Radical Democratic Party of India, held in Bombay during the last week of December 1946, resolved to issue a manifesto incorporating the fundamental principles of New Humanism which it had been developing ever since its foundation six years ago. A statement of these principles in the form of Theses* was adopted by the Conference. In pursuance of the resolution, a draft of the manifesto to be issued was submitted to the Central Political Council of the party which met on May 23rd to 25th, 1947, to discuss the document. The draft being an elaboration of the Theses adopted by the Party Conference, and also of a statement on the international situation issued previously, the Central Political Council of the party approved it on principle. But as author of the draft, I moved that formal endorsement by the Party and publication of the manifesto in its behalf should be deferred yet for some time. The motion was adopted with the proviso that meanwhile the draft should be published, so that it might be considered by progressive opinion throughout the world. It is, however, not a statement of my personal view. The original draft prepared by me has been considerably improved thanks to valuable suggestions from others. Philip Spratt, Sikander Choudhury and V. M. Tarkunde should be particularly mentioned.

---

*See Appendix A.

On the whole, the philosophical principles, social doctrines, political theories, as well as the view of the world situation stated in this publication, have been developed over a period of a number of years, by a group of critical Marxists and former Communists. Differentiating themselves from the nationalists, on the one hand, and the orthodox Communists. on the other, they founded the Radical Democratic Party in 1940. Though the break took place, immediately, on the issue of the Second World War, the differences on both the sides were fundamental, involving philosophical and ethical questions underlying political theories and practice. From that fundamental point of view, there was little real difference between Nationalism and Communism, adherents of the latter cult, particularly in India, having taken up a purely nationalist attitude towards the immediate issue of the War.

During the earlier years of the War, the Radicals in India were isolated from the rest of the world. Later on, as soon as the isolation was partially broken, we discovered that others abroad had been also moving towards a new social and political orientation. Welcoming the tendency, which represented the spirit of the time, we however felt that a new orientation as regards political practice and economic reconstruction did not fully meet the requirements of the contemporary world. It was experiencing a crisis of culture which called for a new attitude to life as a whole—a new social ideology, a new philosophy.

This is a modest contribution to that great human effort of our age. While the Theses on the Principles of

Radical Democracy are the central theme of this Manifesto, the background material is to be found in my books, *New Orientation* and *Beyond Communism.*

Dehradun,
15th August, 1947. M. N. ROY

PREFACE

TO THE SECOND EDITION

Since this Manifesto was issued in August 1947, the Fourth All-India Conference of the Radical Democratic Party, held in Calcutta at the end of December 1948, resolved to cease functioning as a political organisation and transform itself into the Radical Humanist Movement. The resolution logically followed from a further clarification and crystallisation of the ideas first outlined in the Theses on the Principles of Radical Democracy, adopted by the Third Party Conference and then elaborated in the Manifesto. The Theses and text of the resolution are added as appendices to this second edition of the Manifesto as background material. Articles 19 and 20 of the Theses and the last three paragraphs of the Manifesto have been amended according to the resolution dissolving the Radical Democratic Party. The original versions are also given in footnotes.

The First Convention of the Radical Humanist Movement was held in Calcutta early in February 1951, to issue two statements on the theory and practice of politics and economics, deduced from the philosophy of New Humanism. My speech explaining those statements is also added as an appendix to this second edition. It outlines a social philosophy which must be developed on the basis of a humanist philosophy of history. An attempt at a humanist interpretation of history from the dawn of civilisation has been made in my book *Reason, Romanticism and Revolution* the first volume of which has been out and the second volume to be published in the near future.

Finally, it may be pointed out that the principles of a humanist philosophy of history and society outlined in the Theses (Appendix A) are deducible only from a general philosophy of nature and life, still to be elaborated on the basis of cosmological, ontological, epistemological and ethical concepts and propositions which are also stated in the Theses. In the Indian Renaissance Institute Summer Camp for Higher Studies of 1949, these different aspects of the philosophical foundation of New Humanism were discussed. My inaugural address on that occasion is added as an appendix (C).

Though presented here as a political philosophy, New Humanism is meant to be a complete system. Based on the ever expanding totality of scientific knowledge, it cannot indeed be a closed system. It will not be a dogmatic system claiming finality and infallibility. It will be a logical integration of the knowledge about the various aspects of existence, showing how it is in the nature of man to be rational and moral, and therefore capable of building a free, harmonious and just social order.

Dehradun.
April, 1953.

M. N. ROY

1

Since the Communist Manifesto

One hundred years have passed since the Communist Manifesto was issued to herald the age of proletarian revolution. It invoked the spectre of Communism stalking over Europe, striking terror in the heart of the bourgeoisie, still in the process of rising. Hardly a realistic picture then, ironically enough, it is, in a way. true to-day. Heralded as the salvation of the civilised world, tortured and tormented by capitalist exploitation, Communism, in practice, has come to be a spectre, terrifying not only the bourgeoisie;. it is causing grave misgivings even amongst the progressive forces of the modern world, who feel very keenly the urgent need for a radical readjustment of political and economic relations, but at the same time cherish cultural values as the most precious heritage of humanity, not to be carelessly, if not callously, lost in the stormy sea of a social revolution.

Is it an irony of history or an irony of fate? Whatever it may be, it is due to the fact that the era of proletarian revolution, heralded a century ago with so much fanfare and prophetic confidence, never came. Nearly three-quarters of a century lapsed before the confidently expected revolution took place in one country, more or less on the prescribed pattern. But it did not spread, to become the world revolution; and the post-revolutionary developments in Russia were not reassuring; they did not move towards the utopia depicted in the Communist Manifesto. Even previously, the picture of the proletarian revolution had lost its original moral appeal and the glamour of humanist romanticism. Its success in one country pragmatically proved that the new order was not to be a creation of man rising as Prometheus unbound; that human creativeness, in the intellectual, moral and cultural fields, was not to be unfettered; that the new order was to enshrine the collective ego of the proletariat, to claim subordination and sacrifice of individuals composing the class.

The result of the miscarriage was a gigantic tragedy. When at last the era of proletarian revolution appeared to begin, it turned out to be a period of triumphant reaction—an era of counter-revolution. That was, indeed, an irony of history.

The Communist Manifesto had proclaimed that human history was to begin with the triumph of the proletarian revolution. Until then, it was "pre-history", man having, through the ages, lived in the bondage of class-ridden society. The era of the proletarian revolution was to culminate in a world revolution, which would at last usher in the history of a free mankind—an inspiring, though rather erroneous, view of history. However, the first proletarian revolution did not lead to the expected world revolution. History did not begin. Still lingering in the "pre-historic" age, governed by the law of the jungle, the civilised world appears to be nearing its end. A third world war, which will certainly be so much more destructive than the previous ones, within half a century, could not have any other consequence.

The First World War was precipitated by the contradictions of capitalism and rivalry of the imperialist powers. It made the belated beginning of the proletarian revolution possible. Thereafter, Marxian dialectics came into operation, as it were with a vengeance. Fascism rose as the antithesis of Communism: the Second World War might have been destined to be the negation of the negation; but actually it created a situation which is heading towards another world war. The international situation is not only drifting to that dangerous direction; those who were expected to be the saviours of a war-torn world, are themselves recklessly pushing it to the very brink of the precipice.

The era of proletarian revolution heralded by the Communist Manifesto, and believed to have been actually inaugurated by the Russian Revolution, has thus opened up the perspective not of a higher civilisation: the perspective is positively apocalyptic. Has the optimism of a whole century been a day-dream, to end in a grand frustration? Or was it all a nightmare?

2

Inadequacy of Current Ideologies

ALL THOUGHTFUL BELIEVERS IN A FUTURE OF HUMANITY must be deeply perturbed by the gloomy perspective. But they must not simply stand aghast, paralysed by the feeling of helplessness amounting to fatalism. They must think furiously so as to lay bare the cause of the malady threatening the very existence of the civilised world, and act boldly to exterminate the cause.

To begin with, the voice of reason must be raised, warning the progressive world against the different varieties of orthodoxy and blind passion, which are creating an atmosphere of stark madness. It is singularly thoughtless and almost criminally irresponsible to take the fatalistic view that yet another war is inevitable, and to hold that it will finally dissolve the old world and clear the ground for a new. This view may be according to the Marxist doctrine of economic determinism. In reality, it betrays a woeful ignorance of the dynamics of human culture, and represents cynicism of the unfounded conviction that the so-called "pre-history" is bound to be ruled by the law of the jungle.

If the final triumph of world revolution was conditional upon yet another war, then, the fanatical forces of revolution must be heading towards a pyrrhic victory.

One does not require a very high degree of imaginativeness to realise that another world war will have the most disastrous consequences, most probably amounting to a complete breakdown of modern civilisation. The greatest possible efforts must be made to head off that threatening catastrophe. The object can be attained only by replacing antiquated political doctrines and theoretical postulates about a utopia which history has mercilessly exploded. Neither the so-called western democracy nor Russian Communism can head off another war, towards which the world is drifting, as it were, by fate. None of the rivals provides a sufficiently inspiring leadership, capable of taking the contemporary world out of the crisis. One has only a threadbare institutionalism to offer as the panacea for all evils; the other, on the contrary, still holds out an ideal which, in the process of realisation, has lost all the glamour of utopia, and appears to be repelling for all who fought to free the world from totalitarian power and spiritual regimentation.

The progressive world, which still pursues the ideals of democratic freedom and economic equalitarianism, and cherishes the human heritage of cultural values, is torn between the two rivals for the leadership of the post-war world. In the absence of a common code of behaviour and standard of values, there can be no unity of purpose, and therefore no co-operation. The result is the present atmosphere of tormenting doubts, corroding suspicions, cynical efforts to stab each other in the back, and the general instability and fear of an impending catastrophe. In this gravest crisis of its entire history, the civilised world needs a new hope, a new faith, a new ideal—a new philosophy of revolutionary theory and practice suitable for the conditions of the time.

For the moment, the tragedy appears to be inevitable. The drama of post-war Europe seems to be unfolding with the inexorable fatality of the Greek tragedy. On the one hand, wedded to the dogma of dictatorship by a monolithic party, which may be camouflaged for tactical reasons, the Communists in Russia and their satellites abroad simply would not believe in the *bona fides* of others who hold that Socialism could be established democratically. On the other hand, honestly progressive elements throughout Europe, who have lost faith in the capitalistic order, and are therefore ready to co-operate in the building of a new society, are repelled by the idea of dictatorship, particularly after having suffered and sacrificed so much in the bitter struggle against Fascism. Nor would the numerous army of confirmed Socialists in the countries with a democratic tradition countenance any kind of dictatorship. There does not seem to be any hope of a synthesis or reconciliation of the conflicting views.

The political history of Europe during the last quarter of a century and more was embittered by an endless recrimination between the Social-Democratic and Communist Parties. The regrettable tradition cannot be obliterated. It was not a superficial difference. The notions of democracy and dictatorship are mutually exclusive: they are logically associated with conflicting philosophies and antithetical codes of cithics and social behaviour.

Drawing inspiration from the Humanist tradition, the democratic Socialists or Social-Democrats visualised social organisation as a harmony of voluntary individual efforts. The free individual discharges his social functions, not under any compulsion, nor again as a homage to the exacting god of a collective ego, but out of a moral conviction which grows from the consciousness of freedom. The idea of dictatorship, on the contrary, marks a complete break with that cultural heritage of modern civilisation. It is a negation of all the social and ethical values which have given expression to the liberating urge of mankind ever since the Man of the Renaissance rose in revolt against spiritual regimentation under the banner of the Christian Church, and temporal totalitarianism of the Holy Roman Empire. That being the case, a reconciliation of the two ideologies, which are dividing the world in antagonistic camps, is not possible. Nor can the one eventually overwhelm the other by winning the loyalty of a decisive majority. Because both are defective, much too inadequate to meet the requirements of the contemporary world. Both have been discredited in experience.

The theory and practice of dictatorship, even as the means to a laudable end, are repugnant. But, on the other hand, the limitations of parliamentary democracy can no longer be ignored. Under it, civil liberties can be reduced to mere formalities. Without accepting the Marxist view that parliamentary democracy is also a class dictatorship, a view which cannot be easily disposed of, critical students of modern history should be able to see that the inadequacies of parliamentary democracy are inherent in itself. In the highly complicated modern industrial society, individual citizens, particularly those belonging to the majority labouring under economic disadvantages, have very little chance of exercising effectively the sovereign right which formally belongs to them. Law gives them little protection, particularly in critical times. It is an indisputable fact that, under the parliamentary system, democracy cannot control the executive. Between two elections, it is completely out of the picture. During that period, a party having a majority in the parliament can constitutionally assume dictatorial power. The guarantee against such a possible abuse of power, with democratic sanction, is not legal. It is provided by the moral sense of the majority party Thus, formal parliamentarism, as such, cannot defend democracy and guarantee civil liberties under all circumstances. Not only a Hitler rose to power "democratically"; the history of the last quarter of a century records the experience of many a country where dictatorships claimed democratic sanction, though they kicked off the ladder after having attained power.

The fundamental defect of parliamentary democracy results from the contradiction between the philosophy and the political practice of Liberalism. While, true to its Humanist tradition, Liberalism proclaimed freedom of the individual, the economic doctrine of *laisser faire*, with its political corollary, place the individual in a helpless position in the wilderness of cut-throat competition. In such circumstances, the political and social practice of Liberalism having negativated the moral excellence of its philosophy, parliamentary democracy was bound to be discredited. If that was not the case, the stormy rise of Fascism could not be rationally explained.

Fascism grew out of the crisis of parliamentary democracy, within the limits of which the social and economic problems confronting Europe in the inter-war period could not be solved. In order to survive Fascism. democracy must outgrow the limitations of formal parliamentarism based on an atomised and therefore helpless electorate. An organised democracy, in a position to wield standing control of the State, should be the political foundation of the new social order. By reorientating itself to this direction, the democratic view of life will open up before modern progressive humanity a new vista of political and economic reconstruction, which will neither postulate an indefinite period of blood and tears, nor be clouded by doubts about the alternative course of peaceful development.

The store of cultural values piled up since the dawn of civilisation is far from being exhausted. The precious heritage of the past provides a solid foundation for a magnificent structure of the future, dreamt alike by revolutionaries and romanticists, utopians and idealists. If the germs of Socialism or Communism grew in the womb of the capitalist society, then, the inspiration for a truly liberating philosophy of the future should also be found in the moral and spiritual values of the so-called bourgeois culture.

3

Degeneration of Communist Theory and Practice

THE ERA OF PROLETARIAN REVOLUTION CONCLUDED WITH the capture of State power by the party of the proletariat in one country. The revolution, on the whole, particularly its constructive aspect, was not according to the Marxist scheme. Even the initial stage was not quite true to the model. If proletarian revolution was to develop according to the Marxist prognosis, it should have happened first in an industrial country like England, rather than in a backwater of the modern world. The Russian Revolution was an accident—result of a fortuitous combination of circumstances. As such, it was itself a negation of the mechanical view of historical determinism. Taking place not necessarily as a part of an *a priori* conceived scheme of historical development, it was not the signal for the world revolution. On the contrary, the hope of the revolution spreading to other countries disappeared, soon thereafter, by 1921.

In Russia, the revolution since then had to sail uncharted seas. Faced with the problem of economic reconstruction, Lenin quickly realised that Marx had written nothing about it. Marxist economic doctrines are all critical. Marx was concerned with the anatomy of capitalism, having for his object to lay bare its contradictions. Then he proceeded to predict that capitalism would, in the fulness of time, break down under its own internal contradictions, and Socialism rise out of its ruins. A prophetic view of history precluded him from planning socialist reconstruction. That was to be determined by the development of the forces of production. Revolution should free them from the fetters of capitalism; thereafter the future would take care of itself. As an economist, Marx was a critic. There is nothing of social engineering or technology in his voluminous writings. Any planning of the future was utopia, which he so severely condemned. While defending his "New Economic Policy", Lenin said that in the works of Marx there was not a word on the economics of Socialism.

Nor did Marx write anything about post-revolutionary political practice. He postulated proletarian dictatorship as the instrument for breaking down the resistance of the dethroned bourgeoisie. What would happen thereafter, how the post-revolutionary society would be politically organised and administered—that again was all left to the operation of the determined and yet incalculable forces of history. He evaded the political issue by setting up the utopia of the State withering away. As regards the problem of economic inter-relations of the new order, he fell back on the anarchist ideal—"from each according to his ability, to each according to his need"—which Lenin characterised as a "useless slogan".

On the authority of the master, the Marxist dictum

has been revised in the Stalin Constitution, which lays down: "From each according to his ability, to each according to his work." If the traditional dictum was a useless slogan, the revision, though apparently a tautological statement, is not necessarily without any meaning; indeed, it has a meaning which justifies inequity and unequal distribution of wealth in the new social order. There is no fair method of evaluating work. The judgment is left to those in power. And it is now known what has been the consequence.

The post-revolutionary political practice and economic reconstruction in Russia have been purely pragmatic. They have no theoretical foundation, no bearing upon the ideological system of Marxism. Therefore it is arbitrary to call them socialist or communist. On the other hand, since the prophet did not prescribe how the new order should be built, nor held out any picture even in broad outlines, the label can be attached to anything, and nobody can prove that the Soviet State and Soviet economy are not communist. The pragmatic reality of the new order cannot be fitted into the hypothetical or imaginary picture which inspired romantic souls in the days of optimism, when the ideal had to be only theoretically justified, its realisation being still in the womb of the future. The discrepancy between the ideal and the reality of the socialist new order cannot but dampen the enthusiasm for it. This disappointing experience has caused heart-searching, particularly on the part of those for whom a mere sequence of events in time is not progress; who look for the significance of the sequence as a decisive factor to guide any judgment of it.

It is no longer a choice between the *status quo* and a social revolution; between the ugly, oppressive, degrading reality of decayed capitalism, reinforcing itself by fascist dictatorship, and the ideal of a new order based on political democracy and economic equality. The choice now is between the ideal of a new order and the new reality of Communism in practice—the Russian Communism.

While previously the choice was simple enough for all advocates of social justice, it is very difficult for independently thinking persons to choose between the alternatives of the post-revolutionary period. Not only has Communism in practice been disappointing; the ideal itself has been put to doubt by experience. Was it worthwhile to pursue an ideal which, at every successive stage of approximation, falls so far short of expectations? At the same time, the status quo became increasingly intolerable; and the need for a new order was felt by a larger number of people with greater keenness. That conflict of emotions in the ranks of revolutionaries precipitated a crisis in the communist movement and its periphery.

Conformism, born of blind faith, could sustain the unthinking fanatic. Others took up the hopeful attitude of wait and see; the disappointing features of the Russian experiment might be matters of emergency; they would disappear as soon as the revolution spread to other countries. But that tolerant attitude of fond expectation could not be maintained when the hope of world revolution vanished in the dreadful atmosphere of triumphant reaction. There was a furious searching of hearts, leading to a differentiation between blind faith, sustained by the hope of monopolist power, and a realistic, intelligent approach to the unforeseen problems of a new situation. The non-proletarian periphery was alienated, seriously weakening the communist movement, which became completely subservient to the pragmatism of the Soviet State. Its function was no longer to promote world revolution, but to do whatever was necessary for the opportunist policy of the new Russian National State, which claimed to be socialist.

The Communist International, forged as the instrument of the coming world revolution, was the first victim of the crisis. It was torn asunder by the contradictions between the problems of pre-revolutionary and post-revolutionary Communisms; between the theory and practice of Communism. By virtue of being the only party in power, the Russian Communists monopolised the leadership of the International. The parties in other countries voluntarily forfeited the freedom of reacting intelligently to the pre-revolutionary conditions under which they had still to operate. The Russian Communists were recognised as the authority not only of communist practice, but also of theory. Pragmatic practice under unforeseen post-revolutionary circumstances provided the sanction for the dogmatic degeneration of the theoretical presuppositions of Marxism. The interest of the State established by the first proletarian revolution militated against the possibility of world revolution. Socialism in one country precluded the realisation of the ideal of international Communism.

The Soviet Republic became a National State—indeed, of a new type—and, as such, was obligatorily drawn into the vortex of international power politics. The Russian experience proved that Socialism or Communism could be nothing more than State Capitalism. The Communist National State of Russia became an integral part of the precarious *status quo*, adding to its precariousness. The antagonism between two types of National States is no less irreconcilable than the antagonism between Capitalism and Socialism, although the conflict of power politics has eclipsed ideological issues. Polarised into two camps, not of revolution and counter-revolution, but of conflicting self-interests of the two types of National States, the world is threatened by another universal total war, which may put an end to civilisation. Is there no way out? Is history going to record the breakdown of yet another civilisation?

We must look beyond the deceptive ideal of Communism, if the threatened catastrophe is to be avoided. We must have faith in human ingenuity and the creativeness of the human mind, which are far from being exhausted. Revolting against the fatalism of the prophetic theoretical system of Karl Marx, the heralds of a new order of social justice must concern themselves with social technology and social engineering, such as would reconcile freedom with planning, autonomy of the individual with the promotion of collective welfare and progress.

4

Liberal Genealogy of Marxism

THE MARXIST ANALYSIS OF CAPITALISM HAS BEEN corroborated by history; but the theory that it would be inevitably replaced by Socialism has proved to be an instance of wishful thinking. The economic interpretation of history has brought Marxism to grief. A philosophy of history, which ignores other factors of human life than the forces of production, particularly the dynamics of ideas, and disregards moral problems, cannot be a reliable guide for constructive social action. Màrxist historicism has been put to test and found wanting. A new, more comprehensive, philosophy of history is the crying need of the day, to show civilised mankind the way out of the crisis. On the other hand, divorced from the economic exigencies of the reality of physical social existence, political theories and moral doctrines are bound to be dogmatic and deceptive.

Originally, the socialist and communist movement did not lack moral fervour. Indeed, the pioneers of the movement denounced the capitalist system for its immorality. The sanction of the demand for a new social order was moral. The ethical connotation of the demand for social justice was palpable. Marx ridiculed his forerunners as utopians, and claimed to have made a science of Socialism. But the emphasis on economic determinism made a teleology out of his essentially scientific view of history. The socialist society was not to be created by men; it was to result automatically and inevitably from the operation of the forces of production: it was to be a necessary product of historcial development. Marxian Socialism claimed the objectivity of science on the ground that, given a knowledge of the laws of history, one could predict with certainty that the capitalist society would give birth to the socialist new order. Marx claimed to have discovered those laws. But no Laplace of social science followed its Newton. Marx himself proved to be a false prophet.

Nevertheless Marx was not the dry-hearted mathematical prophet of history as he has been celebrated by his followers. He was a passionate Humanist; and, with a burning faith in revolution, he was also a romanticist. The idea of revolution is a romantic idea, because it presupposes man's power to remake the world in which he lives. If purposeful human effort is left out of account, social development becomes a mechanistic evolutionary process, making no room for sudden great changes and occasionally accelerated tempo. As the prophet of revolution, Marx was a romanticist. He proclaimed his faith in the creativeness of man which, accelerating the process of social evolution, brought about revolutions. Marx being a Humanist, the force of his theory of revolution was its powerful moral appeal. Even his critics, who do not depart from objectivity, honour Marx for a passionate search for truth and intellectual honesty.

Without a moral fervour of the highest degree, without an intense dislike for injustice, he could not undertake the lone fight to improve the lot of the oppressed and exploited.

One of the most impassioned fighters against cant and hypocrisy, Marx was a great moralist, in the tradition of the ancient prophets of his race. His merciless exposition of the essence of Capitalism was a severe moral condemnation. In the last analysis, *Capital* is a treatise on social ethics—a powerful protest against the servitude of the toiling majority. It may be presumed that Marx abstained deliberately from making the moral appeal of his economic theories explicit, because he hated the cant of the sanctimonious defenders of the established order of inequity. Nevertheless, it was as a moralist that he influenced contemporary history. Only his orthodox followers seem to have been immune to that influence.

Though Marxism has become a totalitarian theory, Marx was an advocate of freedom; and, as a Humanist, he stood for the freedom of the individual. He talked of Socialism as "the kingdom of freedom", where man will be the master of his social environments. One who preached such a Humanist doctrine could not be a worshipper at the shrine of an exacting collective ego, even of the proletariat. According to Marx, under Socialism, human reason will overcome irrational forces which now tyrannise the life of man: as a rational being, man will control his destiny. Freed from the fallacy of economic determinism, the Humanist, libertarian, moralist spirit of Marxism will go into the making of the new faith of our time. It is a part of the accumulated store of human heritage which must be claimed by the builders of the future.

The positive value of Marxism can be appraised only in the context of its liberal tradition. Bernstein was not a revisionist; by pointing out that it was the logical development of Liberalism, he only traced the genealogy of Socialism. The force of his contention that Socialism in practice is organised Liberalism is still to be appreciated. Liberalism proclaimed the principle of individual freedom; but liberal practice nullified the principle by formalising it. Socialism promised the practice of the principle.

His liberal genealogy is most clearly evidenced by the economic doctrines of Marx. The "economic man" is a liberal concept; and it is the point of departure of the Marxian interpretation of history. The labour theory of value is the corner-stone of Marxian economics. It was inherited from Ricardo. The theory of surplus value was a logical deduction from the labour theory of value. The idea of surplus value had, indeed, occurred to early English Socialists, such as Gray, Hodgskin, Thompson and others. On the whole, it cannot be denied that Marx drew upon the doctrines of classical English political economy, which he so severely criticised. His was a truly constructive criticism, the object of which was to free the criticised system of ideas from its fallacies, so that its positive essence might be the foundation of a more advanced theoretical structure. Adam Smith had expressed the view that "the understandings of the greater part of men are necessarily formed by their ordinary employments". The father of bourgeois political economy anticipated the Marxian doctrine that men's ideas are determined by the tools with which they earn their livelihood.

The Marxist attitude towards ethical questions was also of the tradition of bourgeois Utilitarianism. Bentham had declared that sentimental and ascetic morality was of aristocratic origin, and therefore not valid in a different social and cultural atmosphere. The philosophical Radicals approached moral problems from the individualist point of view. They disputed the morality of asking the individual to sacrifice for the interests of society. Deprecating the virtues of obedience and humility, they held that general prosperity and well-being were promoted only by the defence of individual rights and interests. Moral order resulted necessarily from an equilibrium of interests. Running counter to his own Humanist conviction, Marx, however, rejected the liberating doctrine of individualism as a bourgeois abstraction.

Hegelian influence induced Marx to reject the individualist approach to moral problems While the ethical relativism of the Utilitarians was rational, Marxian relativism, notwithstanding its appearance, is dogmatic. being a projection in the future of the Hegelian moral positivism.* In order to establish the dictum that might is right, Hegel rationalised immorality. His positivist ethical doctrine, that there is no moral standard, but that what exists is rational and therefore good, is moral nihilism. There is no difference between the Hegelian positivist doctrine of morality and Marxist relativism in that respect. According to one, the present might is right; projecting the Hegelian doctrine into the future, the other declared coming might to be also right. Hegel said: What is is rational and therefore good: Marx added: The future, as I visualise it, will result inevitably from the present; ergo, it will also be rational and good. In other words, if to-day might is right, it must be so to-morrow as well. The future of Marx has become the present of Communism in power, and the Marxist attitude to moral questions has become positivist.

The Hegelian essence of Marxism as regards ethical problems has been laid bare by the experience of Communists capturing power in one country. There, whatever is. is good; everything done for the defence of the new order is moral; might is right. This Hegelian positivist attitude is not confined to Russia, where the Communists rule; it is shared by the Communists all over the world. The result is moral degeneration of the communist movement, which is therefore losing its appeal for all other rebels against the decayed and disintegrating *status quo*. At the same time, the army of rebels, eager to fight for social justice, is swelling. They come from all classes, particularly the non-proletarian middle strata. Social forces are not polarised as predicted by Marx. The pattern of revolution, therefore, cannot be as prescribed by him.

Unable to outgrow Hegelian innuence, owing to his

fascination for dialectics, Marx broke away from his original moral Radicalism, which, nevertheless, was the strongest appeal of the philosophy of revolution. That essence of Marxism was completely forgotten by its orthodox exponents, who made a political Jesuitism out of their faith.

5

Marxian Theory of Revolution

THE THEORY THAT PRODUCTION OF SURPLUS VALUE IS THE specific feature of Capitalism and represents exploitation of the working class, is the fundamental fallacy not only of Marxist economics, but of the entire philosophy of revolution. The producer not receiving the full value of his labour is not a peculiarity of the capitalist system. Social progress, particularly, development of the means of production, since the dawn of history, has been conditional upon the fact that the entire product, at any time, of the labour of the community was not consumed. The margin can be called social surplus, which has through the ages been the lever of all progress. What is called surplus value in Marxist economic language, is the social surplus produced under Capitalism.

As an extraordinarily penetrating student of economic history, Marx, of course, could not dispute the necessity and progressive social significance of surplus production. Economically, a demand for the abolition of surplus value will be impractical, indeed suicidal. Social surplus will disappear if production of surplus value is ever stopped; then, with the disappearance of the lever of progress, society will stagnate and eventually break down. Ancient civilisations disappeared owing to inadequacy or shrinkage of social surplus.

In expounding this economic theory, Marx maintained that the purpose of capitalist production "is essentially the production of surplus value"; but in that context, he did not expressly suggest its abolition, though that should be done if "exploitation" of labour was ever to cease. A proposal that could not be logically made in the context of an economic theory was, however, made indirectly, when a political doctrine was deduced from it. Blinking at the fact that production of social surplus represents "exploitation" of labour, in the sense that the producer does not get the full value of his labour, and disregarding the consideration that under any economic system, if it is not to stagnate, surplus must be produced, Marx held that under Capitalism production of surplus value represented exploitation of labour because it is appropriated by one class. As a corollary to that fallacious view, he demanded that the class appropriation of social surplus should stop: that expropriation of the expropriators was the condition for the end of exploitation of man by man.

The appropriation of social surplus by one particular class is certainly an undesirable system; it must go. But the sanction for the demand is not economic, but moral; it is a demand for social justice, which however would not result from the Marxist scheme of revolution. This fallacy, logically inherent in Marxist economics and the philosophy of revolution based thereupon, has been exposed pragmatically. It is implicitly admitted in Marxism that even under the socialist economic system social surplus will be produced; and it is explicitly demanded that, for the establishment of Socialism, the expropriator should be expropriated by the proletariat. That evidently means that, under the new order, the social surplus will be appropriated by the new ruling class—the proletariat, pending the advent of the utopia of a classless and stateless society.

Experience should compel rejection of the fallacious philosophy of revolution. Surplus value is produced in the socialist economy of Russia. Otherwise, the much advertised and admired rapid industrial expansion there cannot be explained. Accumulation of capital is the condition *sine qua non;* and that is possible only on the basis of the production of surplus value, that is, production over and above what is actually consumed by the producers. Rapid expansion of industries implies quicker and larger accumulation, which means a broader margin of surplus value. If production of surplus value represents exploitation of labour, then, labour is exploited also under Socialism; and it must be admitted that under the socialist economy of Russia labour is even more exploited—to produce larger surplus value to be accumulated into new capital.

Either one must join Trotsky in the exclamation "Revolution Bertrayed", or come to the conclusion that Socialism is nothing better than State Capitalism. Revolution has not been betrayed; it has been true to the theoretical pattern of Marxism. Its pragmatic practice of reconstruction was logically deduced by Lenin from the theoretical presuppositions of Marxism, as he interpreted them. No, revolution has not been betrayed. It has unfolded itself according to the dogmas of the orthodox neo-Marxism of Lenin and Stalin. The fallacies and inadequacies of the old philosophy of revolution are thus exposed by experience, to inspire efforts for blazing the trail of a new revolutionary philosophy.

The fallacious doctrine of surplus value, and particularly the experience of its appropriation, provided the theoretical foundation of the dogma of class struggle. Marx and his orthodox followers, believing in economic determinism, discovered class struggle throughout history, backwards until the dawn of civilisation. Therefore Marx maintained that the history of civilisation was the history of class struggles. Society undoubtedly was always divided into classes, and the classes had conflicting interests. But at the same time, there was a cohesive tendency, which held society together. Otherwise, it would have disintegrated, time and again, and there would be no social evolution. The refusal of the contemporary capitalist society to be polarised into two classes according to Marxist prediction throws doubt on the theory of class struggle. As regards the past, with some ingenuity, facts may be fitted into any preconceived theoretical pattern.

Marxism certainly is wrong as regards the role of the middle class in the capitalist society. The prophesy that the middle class would disappear in course of time has not been borne out by history. On the contrary, the intellectual and political importance of the middle class proved to be decisive in the critical period ushered in by the first world war. The concentration of the ownership of the means of production in fewer hands necessarily enlarged the middle class. But all those who are deprived of the privileges of capitalist exploitation are not proletarianised. Economically, they may be so described; but in other matters of decisive importance, such as culture and education, they remain a distinct social factor capable of influencing events. As a matter of fact, between capital and labour, the middle class numerically grows, potentially as an enemy of the *status quo*.

Socialism, indeed, is a middle class ideology. Detached from both the antagonistic camps—of capital and labour—and possessed of the requisite intellectual attainments, the middle class alone could produce individuals who saw beyond the clash of immediate economic interests and conceived the possibility of a new order of social justice and harmony. The decay of Capitalism economically ruined the middle class. The result was quickening of their will for the subversion of the *status quo*, which made no place for them. and the striving for a new order. Because of economic destitution, the middle class was prepared to join the proletariat in the fight for Socialism, by which they meant not State Capitalism, but a more equitable social order. They were, however, not culturally proletarianised. They were capable of appreciating cultural and moral values as the positive outcome of human civilisation, and would not sacrifice that precious heritage at the shrine of the revolutionary Providence of economic determinism. The result was a split of the forces of revolution. Marxist dogmatism attached supreme importance to economic considerations. That, together with a cynical attitude to moral and cultural values, alienated the middle class, seriously weakening the forces of revolution intellectually. Selfish economism eclipsed the moral appeal of Socialism.

Lenin saw the mistake of ignoring the middle class, and tried to rectify it, but only in the field of organisation. In theory, the proletariat still remained the chosen people of the Marxist world. Yet, while discussing the organisational problem of the revolutionary party, Lenin admitted that the proletariat by themselves could not develop a social-democratic consciousness, which must be brought to them from outside—by middle-class intellectuals. Emphasising this significant view, Lenin further said that, spontaneously, the working class did not become socialist, but trade-unionist. That revealed the contradiction between Marxist economism and the theory that the proletariat was the builder of the new order.

Lenin generalised his theory: Not only in Russia, but everywhere, the working class was unable to work out an independent ideology; it followed either the bourgeoisie or middle-class socialist intellectuals. That was a clear admission that the ideal of Socialism and the theory of the proletarian revolution were not born out of the experience of the working class; the one was conceived and the other created by middle-class intellectuals. According to Marxism, the emotions and thoughts of the middle-class intellectuals must have been determined by the experience of that class. The glorification of the proletariat as the herald and builder of Socialism was obviously unwarranted. The credit belongs to the middle class, which is so very woefully maligned and totally ignored in the orthodox Marxist scheme of revolution.

Lenin corrected a mistake as regards organisation; but theoretically he was the most intolerant defender of orthodox Marxism. He pointed out the ideological limitations of the proletariat with an entirely different purpose—to expound his theory of party and its role. Since Socialism had to be injected in the proletariat by middle-class intellectuals, the party of the proletariat should be composed of professional revolutionaries who, by the nature of things, could hail only from the middle class. Yet, theoretically, Lenin would not recognise the revolutionary significance of the middle class. The result of his realistic evaluation of the working class was to superimpose the party on the class which it claimed to represent. But in no way was the party a part of the class. It was the self-appointed leader of the class, incorporating its imaginary collective ego. Subsequently, the fascists made much of the "leadership principle". But the dogmatic, uncompromising Marxist Lenin was the theoretician of the principle which came to be the cardinal article of faith of the communist movement.

According to economic determinism, the proletariat must be the most backward class, intellectually and culturally. Only after the establishment of Socialism could the economic conditions of their life improve, and the possibility of intellectual and cultural development be available to them. Disregarding this clear implication of its theoretical presuppositions, Marxism allots to the proletariat the honourable role of leading society towards a higher civilisation. The contradiction is palpable. Communist practice has been vitiated by this theoretical contradiction. A way out of the vicious circle has been found by compelling middle-class intellectuals to sink to the intellectual and cultural level of the proletariat, as the price of the leadership of the party.

There is no intellectual freedom in the communist movement; proud of its proletarian composition, it has no use for the capitalist culture and bourgeois morality. But until now there is no other culture and morality. Proletarian culture is a contradiction in terms; and the cardinal principle of proletarian morality is that everything is fair in love and war; the working class is in the thick of a civil war—the worst of all wars; the end justifies the means. The Communist Party is admittedly amoral, and takes a cynical attitude to cultural values. That is hardly an inspiring leadership for the contemporary world engaged in a struggle for the salvation of the total heritage of human civilisation, which alone can be the foundation of a new order of greater freedom and higher culture. Caught in the throes of a moral crisis, the civilised world is looking out for a better leadership with a more rational attitude towards the problems to be solved, and a nobler philosophy.

The proletariat by itself is not a revolutionary force. The ideal of a new order may have an appeal for it. But intellectual and cultural backwardness does not permit it, as a class, to have a long-distance view. Originally, Marxism took this basic fact into account and set up the doctrine that the historical necessity of revolution was felt by the class-conscious vanguard of the proletariat, which was to constitute the revolutionary party.

The dogma of an uncompromising class struggle, and the false expectation of a polarisation of society into two classes, moved exclusively by economic incentives, led Marx and Lenin, particularly the latter, to visualise revolution taking place through an insurrection engineered by the so-called vanguard of the proletariat, to be followed by its dictatorship over the people. This theory not only defeats its purpose, as proved by the Russian experience, by creating a new system of political domination, cultural regimentation and economic enslavement; but the uniform failure of Communists all over the world, after their accidental success in Russia, proves its utter inadequacy even as a technique for the capture of power.

Scientific inventions since the days of Marx have vastly increased the military might and coercive strength of the existing States, and have rendered the idea of a minority-insurrection impracticable and out of date. On the other hand, by virtue of their class ideology and their failure to offer anything more inspiring than proletarian dictatorship, the Communists were unable to gather together in one movement all the progressive and revolutionary forces; they remained a sectarian and dogmatic body. Even in relation to the proletariat, the Communist Parties failed to attract the culturally more advanced section, which largely remained attached to the older Social-Democratic Parties. Consequently, the revolutionary appeal of Marxism was addressed largely to the most backward strata of society. Finally, Stalin went to the extent of declaring that the unemployed and the unorganised were the most revolutionary social force.

The proletariat could not make the expected revolution; nor did the mystic forces of history unfold themselves cataclysmically, as predicted. But revolution, that is to say, radical reconstruction of society, remains a pressing need of our time, felt by a much larger section of society, and more keenly and consciously, than the proletariat. The urge for a new order is a reaction to the threat for the destruction of the values of civilisation. Naturally, it is felt more acutely by those who can appreciate and cherish those values. But a new philosophy of revolution, suitable for our age, is yet to arise as the beacon light for civilised humanity. The new philosophy must be able to destroy what remains of the moral sanction of the *status quo,* by providing an idea of a new social order to inspire all those disgusted with the present state of affairs. It must also indicate new ways of revolution appropriate to the needs of the time. While the concrete steps for social transformation must differ from place to place in accordance with prevailing conditions, the movement for freedom, if it is to succeed, must outgrow its sectarian class character and be inspired by the humanist spirit and cosmopolitan outlook. It must, further, take the initiative of organising the people into democratic bodies to provide the basis of the post-revolutionary order.

The bourgeoisie versus the proletariat, capital versus labour, is no longer the central issue; indeed, it has never been, although it has been, and still is, an issue to be settled. The conflict of our age is between totalitarianism and democracy, between the all-devouring collective ego —nation or class—and the individual struggling for freedom. Continuation of the capitalist order demands substitution of liberalism by Fascism, in practice, if not as yet in profession. On the other hand, Communism in practice has also established a totalitarian régime, under which all the aspects of life are rigorously regimented. For the moment, the perspective of the fight for freedom looks like the legendary struggle between David and Goliath. But man will once again destroy the Frankenstein of his creation, and tame the Leviathan.

6

A New Political Philosophy

The question of all questions is: Can politics be rationalised? An affirmative answer to this controversial question would not take us very far unless rationalism was differentiated from the metaphysical concept of reason. To replace the teleology of Marxist Materialism by an appeal to the mystical category of reason would not be an advance.

The cognate question is about the relation of politics and morality: Must revolutionary political practice be guided by the Jesuitic dictum—the end justifies the means? The final sanction of revolution being its moral appeal—the appeal for social justice—logically, the answer to the latter question must be in the negative. It is very doubtful if a moral object can ever be attained by immoral means. In critical moments, when larger issues are involved and greater things are at stake, some temporary compromise in behaviour may be permissible. But when practices repugnant to ethical principles and traditional human values are stabilised as the permanent features of the revolutionary regime, the means defeat the end. Therefore communist political practice has not taken the world, not even the working class, anywhere near a new order of freedom and social justice. On the contrary, it has plunged the army of revolution—proletarian as well as non-proletarian—in an intellectual confusion, spiritual chaos, emotional frustration and a general demoralisation.

To overcome this crisis, the fighters for a new world order must turn to the traditions of Humanism and moral Radicalism. The inspiration for a new philosophy of revolution must be drawn from those sources. The nineteenth century Radicals, actuated by the humanist principle of individualism, realised the possibility of a secular rationalism and a rationalist ethics. They applied to the study of man and society the principles and methods of the physical sciences. Positive knowledge of nature—living as well as inanimate—being so much greater to-day than a hundred years ago, the Radical scientific approach to the problems of man's life and inter-relations is bound to be more successful. To-day we can begin with the conviction that it is long since man emerged from the jungle of "pre-history", that social relations can be rationally harmonised, and that therefore appreciation of moral values can be reconciled with efforts for replacing the corrupt and corrosive *status quo* by a new order of democratic freedom. A moral order will result from a rationally organised society, because, viewed in the context of his rise out of the background of a harmonious physical Universe, man is essentially rational and therefore moral. Morality emanates from the rational desire for harmonious and mutually beneficial social relations.

Man did not appear on the earth out of nowhere. He rose out of the background of the physical Universe.

through the long process of biological evolution. The umbilical cord was never broken: man, with his mind, intelligence, will, remains an integral part of the physical Universe. The latter is a cosmos—a law-governed system. Therefore, man's being and becoming, his emotions, will, ideas are also determined: man is essentially rational. The reason in man is an echo of the harmony of the Universe. Morality must be referred back to man's innate rationality. Only then, man can be moral, spontaneously and voluntarily. Reason is only sanction for morality, which is an appeal to conscience, and conscience, in its turn, is the instinctive awareness of, and reaction to, environments. In the last analysis, conscience is nothing mystic or mysterious. It is a biological function, as such mechanistic, on the level of consciousness. The innate rationality of man is the only guarantee of a harmonious order, which will also be a moral order, because morality is a rational function. Therefore, the purpose of all social endeavour should be to make man increasingly conscious of his innate rationality.

Any effort for a reorganisation of society must begin from the unit of society—from the root, so to say. Such an effort to develop a new philosophy of revolution, on the basis of the entire stock of human heritage, and then to elaborate the theory and formulate the principles of the practice of political action and economic reconstruction, therefore, can be called Radicalism.

Radicalism thinks in terms neither of nation nor of class; its concern is man; it conceives freedom as freedom of the individual. Therefore, it can also be called New

Humanism, new, because it is Humanism enriched, reinforced and elaborated by scientific knowledge and social experience gained during the centuries of modern civilisation.

Humanism is cosmopolitan. It does not run after the utopia of internationalism, which presupposes the existence of autonomous National States. The ideal of One World, or a World Government, is not compatible with the continuation of National States. The one makes of the other a pious desire or wishful thinking. A cosmopolitan commonwealth of free men and women is a possibility. It will be a spiritual community, not limited by the boundaries of National States—capitalist, fascist, communist or of any other kind—which will gradually disappear under the impact of cosmopolitan Humanism. That is the Radical perspective of the future of mankind.

7

Radical Democracy

The philosophy which will give modern mankind a new hope and a new faith must put a concrete content into the concept of freedom. If the liberating possibility of social organisation and political institutions is still to be judged by divergent ideological prejudices, discordant doctrines and conflicting dogmas, common efforts for overcoming the present crisis, the greatest in history, and for promoting human progress, will remain a matter of wishful thinking. A common standard of freedom alone can make such common efforts possible.

Quest for freedom can be referred back to man's struggle for existence. It accounts for the triumph of men over nature, in the course of his efforts to satisfy his biological needs. It provides the basis for his constant search for knowledge, which enables him to be progressively free from the tyranny of natural phenomena and physical and social environments. Quest for freedom is a continuation, on a higher level—of intelligence and emotion—of the biological struggle for existence. In modern society, an individual, to be free, must not only be able to enjoy economic sufficiency and security, but live in a social psychological atmosphere free from cultural regimentation and helpful to the development of his intellectual and other human potentialities.

Progressive attainment of freedom in this wide sense by the individuals composing society should provide the criterion for judging the merits of social organisation. Guided by the dictum of ancient wisdom that man is the measure of everything, the philosophy of the future should proclaim that the merit of any pattern of social organisation or political institution is to be judged by the actual measure of freedom it gives to the individual.

Whether it is the nation or a class, any collectivity is composed of individuals. Society is a creation of man—in quest of freedom. Co-operative social relationships were established originally with the purpose of reinforcing the struggle for existence, which the primitive man had undertaken as individual. The quest for freedom is the continuation of the primitive man's struggle for existence. As such, it is the basic urge of all social advancement. Freedom is the progressive elimination of all the factors—physical, social, psychological—which obstruct the unfolding of man's rational, moral and creative potentialities. The function of social relationships should be to secure for individuals, as individuals, the maximum measure of freedom. The sum total of freedom actually enjoyed by its members individually is the measure of the liberating or progressive significance of any social order. Otherwise, the ideals of social liberation and progress are deceptive.

No political philosophy nor a scheme of social reconstruction can have more than a very limited revolutionary significance if it dismisses the concept of individual freedom as an empty abstraction. A political system and an economic experiment, which subordinate the man of flesh and blood to an abstract collective ego, cannot possibly be the suitable means for the attainment of the goal of freedom. It is absurd to argue that negation of freedom is the road to freedom. The purpose of all rational human endeavour, collective as well as individual, should be the attainment of freedom in ever larger measure, and freedom is real only as individual freedom.

A new world of freedom will not result automatically from an economic reorganisation of society. Nor does freedom necessarily follow from the capture of political power by a party claiming to represent the oppressed and exploited classes. The abolition of private property, State-ownership of the means of production, and planned economy do not by themselves end exploitation of labour, nor lead to an equal distribution of wealth. By disregarding individual freedom on the pleas of taking the fullest advantage of technology, of efficiency and collective effort, planned economy defeats its own purpose. Instead of ushering in a higher form of democracy on the basis of economic equality and social justice, it may establish a political dictatorship. Economic democracy is no more possible in the absence of political democracy than the latter is in the absence of the former. That consideration should be borne in mind by those who make a fetish of economic planning.

The crucial question is: planning for what? It is assumed that planned economy will guarantee the greatest good to the greatest number; in other words, it will mean equal distribution of wealth—establish social justice. In that case, it should be possible to reconcile planning with freedom. If modern technological trends preclude such reconciliation, then they should be curbed so as to be more amenable to human welfare. Machine should not be the Frankenstein of modern civilisation. Created by man, it must subserve man's purpose—contribute to his freedom.

Dictatorship of any form, however plausible may be the pretext for it, is excluded by the Radical-Humanist perspective of social evolution. Politics cannot be divorced from ethics without jeopardising the cherished ideal of freedom. It is an empirical truth that immoral means necessarily corrupt the end. In the Soviet Union, proletarian dictatorship promises to be a permanent institution. It has become identical with Communism. The means have become the end. The State does not hold out any hope of withering away. If a socialist society has been established in the Soviet Union, then, the period of transition has passed, and dictatorship must disappear. But so long as no other party is allowed to exist, or the party of the proletariat does not disappear with dictatorship, it is idle to say that a higher form of democracy has been established.

The practice of Western Democracy is equally disappointing. Traditional democratic Socialism, therefore, also does not inspire any confidence of success. Democracy must reorientate itself. It must revert to the humanist tradition. It must not be limited by the counting of heads, particularly when the heads have not.

the opportunity to raise themselves with sovereign dignity. Formal parliamentarism must be replaced by actual democratic practice. The character of a party is to be judged not by its ability to catch votes, but by the merit of its proclaimed principles and published programme. The people should be asked to vote not for professions and promises, but by judging the record of a government. Democratic practice which is no more than mere counting of heads, in the last analysis, is also a homage to the collective ego. It allows scope neither for the individual nor for intelligence. Under the formal parliamentary system, unscrupulous demagogues can always come to the top. Intelligence, integrity, wisdom, moral excellence, as a rule, count for nothing. Yet, unless the purifying influence of these human values is brought to bear upon the political organisation and administration of society, the democratic way of life can never be realised.

The contemporary world is not poor in men and women incorporating those values of the humanist tradition. But disdaining demagogy, they can never come to the helm of public affairs. On the other hand, a dictatorial regime, even if established as the means to a laudable end, discourages the rise of that type of citizens. Thus, between formal democracy and dictatorship, humanity is deprived of the benefit of having its affairs conducted by spiritually free individuals, and is consequently debarred from advancing towards the goal of freedom.

It is idle to condemn dictatorship on the ground

that regimentation precludes the creation of human values, so long as those values are not allowed to influence public affairs even under so-called democratic regimes. To wean the unthinking world away from the appeal of dictatorship, postulated as a short-cut, indeed as the only way to freedom, democracy must recover the humanist tradition of modern culture.

Man must again be the measure of all things. Intelligence, integrity, wisdom, moral excellence, should be the test of leadership. Democracy can no longer be taken simply for granted. To-day all thoughtful lovers of freedom are perturbed by the challenging question: Is democracy possible? The advocates of democratic Socialism, while rightly rejecting dictatorship, have so far failed to answer satisfactorily this question of our time. The fundamental democratic principle—the greatest good to the greatest number—can be realised only when the conduct of public affairs will be in charge of spiritually free individuals who represent their own conscience before anybody or anything else.

Moral sanction, after all, is the greatest sanction. The real guarantee of parliamentary democracy is not law, but the moral conscience of the majority in power. In the last analysis, dictatorship also rests on a moral sanction; it claims to be the means to an end. But group morality is a doubtful guarantee against the temptation of power. Values operate through individuals. Therefore, a government composed of spiritually free individuals, accountable, in the first place, to their respective conscience, is the only possible guarantee for securing the greatest good to the greatest number. Democracy must have that philosophical reorientation, if it is to survive the present crisis and resist the powerful onslaught of dictatorship.

What is suggested is not a rule of the "intellectual élite", but such an organisation of society as will give unlimited scope for the unfolding of the creative genius of man, by placing the executive power of the State under the control of free individuals—free from the influence of vested interests and also from the vagaries of the collective ego, so very susceptible to demagogic appeals. Democratic practice should not be confined to periodical elections. Even if elections are by universal suffrage, and the executive is also elected, democracy will still remain a mere formality. Delegation of power, even for a limited period, stultifies democracy. Government for the people can never be fully a government of the people and by the people.

The people can have a hand in the government only when a pyramidal structure of the State will be raised on a foundation of organised local democracies. The primary function of these latter will be to make individual citizens fully conscious of their sovereign right and enable them to exercise the right intelligently and conscientiously. The broad basis of the democratic State, coinciding with the entire society, will be composed of a network of political schools, so to say. The right of recall and referendum will enable organised local democracies to wield a direct and effective control of the entire State machinery. They alone will have the right to nominate candidates for election. Democracy will be placed above parties. Individual men will have the chance of being recognised, on their merit. Party loyalty and party patronage or other forms of nepotism will no longer eclipse intellectual independence, moral integrity and detached wisdom.

In other words, what is suggested is creation of conditions under which democracy can be possible. In the first place, there must be a conscious and integrated effort to stimulate amongst the people the urge for freedom, the desire to rely upon themselves and to be the makers of their destiny, the spirit of free thinking, and the will never to submit to any external authority by exchanging their freedom for the security of slaves. A new Renaissance, based on rationalism, individualism and cosmopolitan Humanism, is essential for democracy to be realised and capable of defending itself.

Such an atmosphere will foster intellectual independence dedicated to the cause of making human values triumph. Moral excellence alone can mould a community together without sacrificing the individual on the alter of the collective ego, be it of the nation or a class. Men and women, possessed of that great virtue, will command the respect of an intelligent public, and be recognised as the leaders of society. Demagogy will be placed under a heavy discount. Democratic practice will not be reduced to periodical elections. People will no longer be mere "masses".

It will be some time before reorientated democracy can thus be the master of the situation. In the transition period, a democratic Constitution should provide for creative genius, intellectual detachment and moral integrity occupying a high place in the State, so as to advise, guide and influence the operation of executive power. In the transition period, democracy must be elective as well as selective. Until the intellectual and moral level of the entire community is raised considerably, election alone cannot possibly bring its best elements to the fore-front, and unless the available intellectual detachment and moral integrity are brought to bear upon the situation, democracy cannot come to her own.

During the transition period, residuary power should be vested in a Council of State representing men of science, intelligence, integrity, wisdom and moral excellence; men, who, as a rule, keep aloof from the rough and tumble of politics, and therefore are not to be found among professional politicians. The valuable services of those who are the best qualified to be the leaders of society can be enlisted in the following manner:

Each professional group—of engineers, economists, scientists, medical men, jurists, historians and others engaged in intellectual, literary, artistic and any other creative avocation, will recommend a specific number for membership of the Council of State. They will be nominated by the head of the State, who will have the prerogative also to nominate some other persons equally qualified, though not formally attached to any particular group. Any possible indirect control of the vested interests will be obviated by stipulating that members of the professional groups, who are remuneratively connected with profit-making concerns, except as salaried employees, shall not be eligible for the membership of the Council of State. The power of planning the development of society in all branches (economic, health, education, culture) and also to guide and supervise the execution of the plans, will be vested in the Council of State.

To begin with, the economic life of society must be progressively freed from the paralysing and corrupting control of vested interests. In consequence thereof, intellectual independence will be accessible to a greater number. Secondly, these latter should be regarded as the most trustworthy custodians of public welfare, and afforded the opportunity to function as such. If, before democracy has come of age, their intrinsically representative character is to be measured by the counting of heads, society will remain deprived of the best available leadership, which alone can guide it towards true democratic freedom.

Radicalism presupposes economic reorganisation of society, so as to eliminate the possibility of exploitation of man by man. Progressive satisfaction of material necessities is the precondition for the individual members of society unfolding their intellectual and other finer human attributes. An economic reorganisation such as will guarantee a progressively rising standard of living will be the foundation of the Radical Democratic State.

The economy of the new social order will be based

on production for use and distribution with reference to human needs. Its political organisation will exclude delegation of power which in practice deprives the people of effective power. It will be based on the direct participation of the entire adult population through the People's Committees. Its culture will be based on universal dissemination of knowledge and incentive to scientific and all other kinds of creative activity. The new society, being founded on reason and knowledge, will necessarily be planned. But it will be planning with the freedom of the individual as its main objective. The new society will be democratic—politically, economically, as well as culturally. It will be a democracy capable of defending itself.

The ideal of Radical Democracy, will be attained through the collective efforts of spiritually free men and women united with the determination of creating a new order of freedom. They will function as the guides, friends and philosophers of the people rather than as their would-be rulers. Consistent with the goal of freedom, their political practice will be rational and ethical. Their effort will be reinforced by the growth of the people's will to freedom. Ultimately, the Radical Democratic State will rise with the support of enlightened public opinion as well as intelligent action of the people. Realising that freedom is inconsistent with concentration of power, Radical Humanists will not seek to capture power. They will help democracy organise itself in People's Committees, which will eventually become the organs of democratic power. Thus, becoming coterminous with the entire society, the Radical Democratic State, as the organ for its political administration, will cease to be an instrument of coercion. At last, democracy—government of the people and by the people—will be possible.

In the last analysis, education of the citizen is the condition for such a reorganisation of society as will be conducive to common progress and prosperity without encroaching upon the freedom of the individual. The People's Committees will be the school for the political and civic education of the citizen. The structure and function of the Radical Democratic State will enable detached individuals to come to the forefront of public affairs. Manned with such individuals, the State will no longer be the Leviathan, always to be dreaded and distrusted.

The function of a revolutionary and liberating social philosophy is to lay emphasis on the basic fact of history, that man is the maker of his world—man as a thinking being, and he can be so only as an individual. The brain is the means of production, and produces the most revolutionary commodity. Revolutions presuppose iconoclastic ideas. An increasingly large number of men, conscious of their creative power, motivated by an indomitable will to remake the world, moved by the adventure of ideas, and fired with the ideal of a free society of free men, can create conditions under which democracy will be possible. Spiritually free individuals at the helm of affairs will smash all chains of slavery and usher in freedom for all.

NOTE TO CHAPTER 6

In the Original Version of the Manifesto of New Humanism as published in the first edition of this book the paragraphs "The ideal of Radical Democracy . . . . freedom for all" ran as follows :—

The ideal of Radical Democracy will be attained through the collective efforts of spiritually free men and women united in a political party with the determination of creating a new order of freedom. The members of the party will function as the guides, friends and philosophers of the people rather than as their would-be rulers. Consistent with the goal of freedom, the political practice of the party will be rational and ethical. The party will grow with the growth of the people's will to freedom, and help the establishment of the Radical Democratic State with the support of enlightened public opinion as well as intelligent action of the people. Realising that freedom is inconsistent with concentration of power, the party will not seek to capture power. It will help democracy organise itself in People's Committees, which will eventually become the organs of democratic power. Thus, becoming coterminous with the entire society, the State will cease to be an instrument of coercion. At last, democracy—government of the people and by the people—will be possible.

In the last analysis, education of the citizen is the condition for such a reorganisation of society as will be conducive to common progress and prosperity without encroaching upon the freedom of the individual. The Radical Democratic State will be the school for the political and civic education of the citizen. Its structure and function will enable detached individuals to come to the forefront of public affairs. Manned with such individuals, the State will no longer be the Leviathan, always to be dreaded and distrusted.

The function of a revolutionary and liberating social philosophy is to lay emphasis on the basic fact of history that man is the maker of his world—man as a thinking being, and he can be so only as an individual. The brain is a means of production, and produces the most revolutionary commodity. Revolutions presuppose iconoclastic ideas. An increasingly large number of men, conscious of their creative power, motivated by an indomitable will to remake the world, moved by the adventure of ideas, and fired with the ideal of a free society of free men, can create conditions under which democracy will be possible. Spiritually free individuals in power will smash all chains of slavery and usher in freedom for all.

APPENDIX A

PRINCIPLES OF RADICAL DEMOCRACY 22 THESES.

22 THESES

ONE

MAN IS THE ARCHETYPE OF SOCIETY, CO-OPERATIVE SOCIAL relationships contribute to develop individual potentialities. But the development of the individual is the measure of social progress. Collectivity presupposes the existence of individuals. Except as the sum total of freedom and well-being, actually enjoyed by individuals, social liberation and progress are imaginary ideals, which are never attained. Well-being, if it is actual, is enjoyed by individuals. It is wrong to ascribe a collective ego to any form of human community (*viz.*, nation, class, etc.), as that practice means sacrifice of the individual. Collective well-being is a function of the well-being of individuals.

TWO

QUEST FOR FREEDOM AND SEARCH FOR TRUTH CONSTITUTE the basic urge of human progress. The quest for freedom is the continuation, on a higher level—of intelligence and emotion—of the biological struggle for existence. The search for truth is a corollary thereof. Increasing knowledge of nature enables man to be progressively free from the tyranny of natural phenomena, and physical and social environments. Truth is the content of knowledge.

THREE

THE PURPOSE OF ALL RATIONAL HUMAN ENDEAVOUR, INDIVIDUAL as well as collective, is attainment of freedom, in ever increasing measure. Freedom is progressive disappearance of all restrictions on the unfolding of the potentialities of individuals, as human beings, and not as cogs in the wheels of a mechanised social organism. The position of the individual, therefore, is the measure of the progressive and liberating significance of any collective effort or social organisation. The success of any collective endeavour is to be measured by the actual benefit for its constituent units.

Four

Rising out of the background of the law-governed physical nature, the human being is essentially rational. Reason being a biological property, it is not the antithesis of will. Intelligence and emotion can be reduced to a common biological denominator. Historical determinism, therefore, does not exclude freedom of the will. As a matter of fact, human will is the most powerful determining factor. Otherwise, there would be no room for revolutions in a rationally determined process of history. The rational and scientific concept of determinism is not to be confused with the teleological or religious doctrine of predestination

Five

The economic interpretation of history is deduced from a wrong interpretation of Materialism. It implies dualism, whereas Materialism is a monistic philosophy. History is a determined process; but there are more than one causative factors. Human will is one of them, and it cannot always be referred directly to any economic incentive.

Six

IDEATION IS A PHYSIOLOGICAL PROCESS RESULTING FROM the awareness of environments. But once they are formed, ideas exist by themselves, governed by their own laws. The dynamics of ideas runs parallel to the process of social evolution, the two influencing each other mutually. But in no particular point of the process of the integral human evolution, can a direct causal relation be established between historical events and the movements of ideas. ('Idea' is here used in the common philosophical sense of ideology or system of ideas). Cultural patterns and ethical values are not mere ideological super-structures of established economic relations. They are also historically determined—by the logic of the history of ideas.

Seven

FOR CREATING A NEW WORLD OF FREEDOM, REVOLUTION must go beyond an economic reorganisation of society. Freedom does not necessarily follow from the capture of political power in the name of the oppressed and exploited classes and abolition of private property in the means of production.

Eight

COMMUNISM OR SOCIALISM MAY CONCEIVABLY BE THE means for the attainment of the goal of freedom. How far it can serve that purpose, must be judged by experience. A political system and an economic experiment which subordinate the man of flesh and blood to an imaginary collective ego, be it the nation or a class, cannot possibly be the suitable means for the attainment of the goal of freedom. On the one hand, it is absurd to argue that negation of freedom will lead to freedom; and, on the other hand, it is not freedom to sacrifice the individual at the altar of an imaginary collective ego. Any social philosophy or scheme of social reconstruction which does not recognise the sovereignty of the individual, and dismisses the ideal of freedom as an empty abstraction, can have no more than a very limited progressive and revolutionary significance.

Nine

The State being the political organisation of society, its withering away under Communism is a utopia which has been exploded by experience. Planned economy on the basis of socialised industries presupposes a powerful political machinery. Democratic control of that machinery alone can guarantee freedom under the new order. Planning of production for use is possible on the basis of political democracy and individual freedom.

Ten

State ownership and planned economy do not by themselves end exploitation of labour; nor do they necessarily lead to an equal distribution of wealth. Economic democracy is no more possible in the absence of political democracy than the latter is in the absence of the former.

ELEVEN

DICTATORSHIP TENDS TO PERPETUATE ITSELF. PLANNED economy under political dictatorship disregards individual freedom on the pleas of efficiency, collective effort and social progress. Consequently, a higher form of democracy in the socialist society, as it is conceived at present, becomes an impossibility. Dictatorship defeats its professed end.

TWELVE

THE DEFECTS OF FORMAL PARLIAMENTARY DEMOCRACY HAVE also been exposed in experience. They result from the delegation of power. To make democracy effective, power must always remain vested in the people, and there must be ways and means for the people to wield the sovereign power effectively, not periodically, but from day to day. Atomised individual citizens are powerless for all practical purposes, and most of the time. They have no means to exercise their sovereignty and to wield a standing control of the State machinery.

THIRTEEN

LIBERALISM IS FALSIFIED OR PARODIED UNDER FORMAL parliamentary democracy. The doctrine of *laissez faire* only provides the legal sanction to the exploitation of man by man. The concept of economic man negativates the liberating doctrine of individualism. The economic man is bound to be a slave or a slave-holder. This vulgar concept must be replaced by the reality of an instinctively rational being who is moral because he is rational. Morality is an appeal to conscience, and and conscience is the instinctive awareness of, and reaction to, environments. It is a mechanistic biological function on the level of consciousness. Therefore, it is rational.

FOURTEEN

THE ALTERNATIVE TO PARLIAMENTARY DEMOCRACY IS NOT dictatorship; it is organised democracy in the place of the formal democracy of powerless atomised individual citizens. The parliament should be the apex of a pyramidal structure of the State reared on the base of an organised democracy composed of a countrywide network of People's Committees. The political organisation of society (the State) will be coincident with the entire society, and consequently the State will be under a standing democratic control.

FIFTEEN

THE FUNCTION OF A REVOLUTIONARY AND LIBERATING social philosophy is to lay emphasis on the basic fact of history that man is the maker of his world—man as a thinking being, and he can be so only as an individual. The brain is a means of production, and produces the most revolutionary commodity. Revolutions presuppose iconoclastic ideas. An increasingly large number of men conscious of their creative power, motivated by the indomitable will to remake the world, moved by the adventure of ideas, and fired with the ideal of a free society of free men, can create the conditions under which democracy will be possible.

SIXTEEN

THE METHOD AND PROGRAMME OF SOCIAL REVOLUTION must be based on a reassertion of the basic principle of social progress. A social renaissance can come only through determined and widespread endeavour to educate the people as regards the principles of freedom and rational co-operative living. The people will be organised into effective democratic bodies to build up the socio-political foundation of the post revolutionary order. Social revolution requires in rapidly increasing number men of the new renaissance, and a rapidly expanding system of People's Committees, and an organic co-ordination of both. The programme of revolution will similarly be based on the principles of freedom, reason and social harmony. It will mean elimination of every form of monopoly and vested interest in the regulation of social life.

SEVENTEEN

RADICAL DEMOCRACY PRESUPPOSES ECONOMIC REORGANISation of society so as to eliminate the possibility of exploitation of man by man. Progressive satisfaction of material necessities is the precondition for the individual members of society unfolding their intellectual and other finer human potentialities. An economic reorganisation, such as will guarantee a progressively rising standard of living, is the foundation of the Radical Democratic State. Economic liberation of the masses is an essential condition for their advancing towards the goal of freedom.

Eighteen

The economy of the new social order will be based on production for use and distribution with reference to human needs. Its political organisation excludes delegation of power which in practice, deprives the people of effective power; it will be based on the direct participation of the entire adult population through the People's Committees. Its culture will be based on universal dissemination of knowledge and on minimum control and maximum scope for, and incentive to, scientific and creative activities. The new society, being founded on reason and science, will necessarily be planned. But it will be planning with the freedom of the individual as its main purpose. The new society will be democratic—politically, economically as well as culturally. Consequently, it will be a democracy which can defend itself.

Nineteen

The ideal of Radical Democracy will be attained through the collective efforts of spiritually free men united in the determination of creating a world of freedom. They will function as the guides, friends and philosophers of the people rather than as their would-be rulers. Consistently with the goal of freedom, their political practice will be rational and therefore ethical. Their effort will be reinforced by the growth of the people's will to freedom. Ultimately, the Radical Democratic State will rise with the support of enlightened public opinion as well as intelligent action of the people. Realising that freedom is inconsistent with concentration of power, Radical Democrats will aim at the widest diffusion of power.

TWENTY

IN THE LAST ANALYSIS, EDUCATION OF THE CITIZEN IS THE condition for such a reorganisation of society as will be conducive to common progress and prosperity without encroaching upon the freedom of the individual. The People's Committees will be the schools for the political and civic education of the citizen. The structure and function of the Radical Democratic State will enable detached individuals to come to the forefront of public affairs. Manned with such individuals, the State machinery will cease to be the instrument in the hands of any particular class to coerce others. Only spiritually free individuals in power can smash all chains of slavery and usher in freedom for all.

TWENTYONE

RADICALISM INTEGRATES SCIENCE INTO SOCIAL ORGANISation and reconciles individuality with collective life; it gives to freedom a moral-intellectual as well as a social content; it offers a comprehensive theory of social progress in which both the dialectics of economic determinism and dynamics of ideas find their due recognition; and it deduces from the same a method and a programme of social revolution in our time.

Twentytwo

Radicalism starts from the dictum that "man is the measure of everything" (Protagoras) or "man is the root of mankind" (Marx), and advocates reconstruction of the world as a commonwealth and fraternity of free men, by the collective endeavour of spiritually emancipated moral men.

NOTE TO APPENDIX A

In the original version of the "Principles of Radical Democracy" as published in the first edition, Theses 19 and 20 ran as follows :

NINTEEN

The ideal of Radical Democracy will be attained through the collective efforts of spiritually free men united in a political party with the determination of creating a world of freedom. The members of the party will function as the guides, friends and philosophers of the people rather than as their would-be rulers. Consistently with the goal of freedom, the political practice of the party will be rational and therefore ethical. The party will grow with the growth of the people's will to freedom, and come to power with the support of enlightened public opinion as well as intelligent action of the people. Realising that freedom is inconsistent with concentration of power, its aim will be the widest diffusion of power. Its success in attaining political power will only be a stage in that process, and by the logic of its own existence, the party will utilise political power for its further diffusion until the State becomes coterminous with the entire society.

TWENTY

In the last analysis, education of the citizen is the condition for such a reorganisation of society as will be conducive to common progress and prosperity without encroaching upon the freedom of the individual. The Radical Democratic State will be the school for the political and civic education of the citizen. Its structure and function will enable detached individuals to come to the forefront of public affairs. Manned with such individuals, the State machinery will cease to be the instrument in the hands of any particular class to coerce others. Only spiritually free individuals in power can smash all chains of slavery and usher in freedom for all.

APPENDIX B

PRACTICE OF NEW HUMANISM

Practice of New Humanism

Statement adopted by the All-India Conference of the Radical Democratic Party held in Calcutta, 26th to 30th December, 1948.

Two years ago, in the last All-India Conference, the Radical Democratic Party adopted the Fundamental Principles of New Humanism in the form of 22 Theses. Those philosophical principles and their political deductions were formulated in an effort to offer a solution of the crisis in which the contemporary world has been involved ever since the termination of hostilities in the last war. The main features of the crisis have become more prominent and obvious now. But they were already discernible two years ago. Developments which have taken place during the intervening period have confirmed our conclusions both with regard to the nature of the problem as well as its possible solution.

If the principles of New Humanism measure up to the nature and gravity of the world crisis, it follows that the practice of those principles would offer the most plausible solution of that crisis. Doubts on the practice of New Humanism are themselves the symptoms of the disease which it seeks to cure. They arise from traditional notions about politics and political activity, as well as the traditional attitude which regards the common people as mere tools of one or the other political party.

Politics of the traditional type has lost all progressive significance. Political theory and practice are still conceived in terms of a situation which has ceased to exist. Capitalism is no longer a stable social order claiming adherence on its own merits. In large parts of the world, it has already collapsed, and almost everywhere it has lost its moral sanction. The consequent social instability has created a new situation. On the one hand, large masses of people affected by a sense of insecurity have become more amenable to the appeal of totalitarianism, whether in the name of the nation or the class. They are prone to exchange their individuality, their existence as free thinking beings, for the false sense of security and power acquired by merging into a collectivity. On the other hand, with the collapse of capitalism, social leadership has gradually shifted from the owners of capital to the leaders of successful political parties. The result is the predominance of power-politics. The process is aided by a third factor. With the end of competitive capitalism, the doctrine of *laisser faire* has been replaced by that of State planning. Economic planning increases the scope and power of the State. Those in control of the State are placed in possession of a vast concentration of power. The prize of power-politics is the establishment of a formidable dictatorship.

It is hardly an exaggeration to say that the era of capitalism is giving place to the era of power-politics. The political world is being polarised not between the supporters and opponents of capitalism, but between totalitarian forces thirsting for dictatorial power. Whether they emerge from the right or the left, is immaterial to the final outcome. The triumph of either is equally harmful to the cause of freedom, democracy and general well-being. Therefore, the issue is no longer between capitalism and socialism, but between dictatorship resulting from power-politics and democracy. In this situation, traditional concepts of politics must be given up; democratic politics must be conceived differently.

Leftist parties with a socialist programme, even when they profess to be democratic, offer no solution to the crisis of our time. In the first place, the programme of nationalisation of the means of production, distribution and exchange takes no notice of the central problem of today, which is how to make democracy a reality. Consequently, in the context of the present situation, their programme tends to be similar to that of the parties of the right. Private capitalism, *laisser faire* economy, having proved untenable, the rightists also stand for State planning, which means State control over the means of production, distribution and exchange. Moreover, neither of the champions of State control offer any remedy against the concentration of power which their programme involves. Both are wedded to parliamentary democracy, which enables a political minority to rule in the name of the people, and makes of popular sovereignty a mere formality. Economic control by the State has no liberating value in the absence of political control of the State by the people. Wedded to parliamentary democracy, socialism is indistinguishable from State capitalism.

More significant than the similarity in the leftist and rightist programme is the similarity in their political practice. Engaged in a struggle for power, they tend to adopt means which contradict their profession of democracy. Striving to become popular, they tend to flatter the prejudices of the people and foster the authoritarian tradition rooted in their cultural and political backwardness. While democracy presupposes a self-reliant people, conscious of their rationality and individual dignity, leftist parties no less than the rightist seek to rely on totalitarian sentiments. To the collectivist appeal of the class, they add the totalitarian appeal of the nation. Socialists thus become the champions of nationalism. No difference being thus left in the programme as well as the political practice of various parties, the struggle between them assumes the character of a mere scramble for power, which is not only devoid of any progressive possibility, but is destructive of the cultural values of democracy. It has aided the growth of totalitarian forces in different countries and brought the world to the verge of a catastrophic military conflict.

Pursuit of power, even when undertaken as a means to its diffusion, defeats the purpose. In the sphere of power-politics, that party succeeds which excels others in its totalitarian appeal and in the complementary qualities of demagogy, blind faith and hero-worship. No party which joins in the struggle can win and yet remain democratic either in its internal organisation or in its attitude to, and influence on, the people.

Consequently, once power is captured by any party, it is never diffused.

The growth of totalitarianism in politics has synchronised with the growth of irrationalism and neo-mysticism in natural and social philosophy, and of teleological views in history and politics. Faith in the creativity of man has been overwhelmed by the sense of his ignorance and helplessness. There has been a reversion from the humanist tradition of the European Renaissance, which had within a comparatively short period brought about an unparalleled advance in man's quest for freedom. The relapse of the West from the values of individualism, rationalism and humanism has found a sympathetic echo in the tradition of fatalism and blind faith already prevailing in eastern countries like India, which have yet to undergo the experience of a Renaissance. The result has been a general lack of confidence in the ability of man to control the forces generated by his own ingenuity in science and technology.

The lack of confidence in the ability of the common people to manage public affairs has found political expression in the replacement of monarchy by the so-called representative government. The parliamentary practice of the delegation of power nullifies the principle that sovereignty belongs to the people. Those who oppose parliamentary democracy from the left also start from the pseudo-scientific assumption that the intellectual and moral advancement of the people, which is necessary for the establishment of democracy, is impossible in the absence of an improvement in their economic conditions to be brought about by a minority in power. These views furnish the sanction for power-politics and provide the pretext of a benevolent dictatorship. On the other hand once established, any dictatorship tends to perpetuate itself. Those who rule do not adopt measures to destroy the basis of their rule. The result is complete helplessness of the people.

Democracy can be established only by the reassertion of the humanist tradition. Man is the measure of his world. Being inherently rational, he can always learn from experience. He develops his intellectual faculties and moral values in his efforts to secure a better life for himself. That ability is not confined to a few, nor acquired at a particular economic level. While economic sufficiency may be helpful to cultural growth, the view that the one is the precondition of the other is historically false and logically untenable. Man's faculties have developed in the course of his struggle for existence.

Throughout the course of history, spiritual revolts have always preceded great social changes. Mental freedom has necessarily been the precondition for any attempt to attain political and economic freedom. Faced with economic insufficiency, political oppression and social instability, the people can nevertheless develop the will as well as the ability to change that situation. Scientific Humanism precludes the view that the will to freedom and the ability to attain it are accessible only to a minority, which is thus qualified for leadership.

A survey of the main features of the contemporary crisis reinforces the conclusion already reached by Radical Democrats, that a political party striving for power cannot be the means to the attainment of freedom. A movement for freedom as visualised in the philosophy of New Humanism must be broader than a political movement, nor can it be organised and led by a political party of the traditional type. Standing outside the scramble for power, it will seek to educate people in the cultural values essential for the realisation of democracy. Creation of a new outlook of life will be its primary function and, in the conditions prevailing in India, its major preoccupation for some length of time. On that basis, it will develop democratic institutions which will bring about the widest diffusion of power. The impact of its ideas will not be limited to political and economic spheres. It will result in the rise of new men and women engaged in the task of establishing new form of social relations and building new patterns of political institutions. The movement will be a comprehensive, intellectual-social movement.

Committed to the pursuit of scientific politics, the Radical Democratic Party has already been developing into such a broad movement. The party has from its inception concentrated on the political education of the people, confined itself to rational propaganda, and never compromised its views in the interests of power-politics. It has already laid the foundation of a Renaissance movement. It has developed the concept of organised democracy, in which power will not be delegated by the people to a political party, but will remain vested in the people, who will be able to wield it from day to day by participating in political administration. Finally, realising that power, except when it is actually vested in the people, is the negation of freedom, the party has abjured the aim of coming to power, which was inconsistent with its theory, and was conceived only under the influence of traditional notions. With these changes, it has been outgrowing the original pattern of a traditional political party.

In order to complete this process, the Radical Democrats will reorganise themselves. so as to develop more effectively a comprehensive social movement inspired by the philosophy of New Humanism and this will henceforth be known as the Radical Humanist movement. This will signify, on the one hand, changes in the programme of the Radicals and in their day-to-day activities. On the other hand, the adoption of a more appropriate name will indicate the comprehensive nature of the movement and will also free it from the notions associated with the aim, activity and organisation of political parties. The work and progress of the Radical Humanist Movement will no longer be judged in terms of mass following, but by the spread of the spirit of freedom, rationality and secular morality amongst the people, and in the increase of their influence in the State.

The programme of the Radical Humanist Movement will be to strive for such a reconstruction of society as will progressively eliminate the impediments, economic or cultural, to the full development of the human personality.

The political organisation of the new society has already been outlined in the 22 Theses adopted by the last Party conference, and illustrate in the draft constitution of Free India sponsored by the Radical Democratic Party four years ago. The State will be an organised democracy in which the people as a whole will exercise standing control and constant supervision over the legislative and executive functions of the State. The Parliament will be the apex of a pyramidal structure based on a net-work of people's committees functioning as schools of political education of the people as well as organs of popular sovereignty. The State will be manned by spiritually free men and women possessed of intellectual integrity and moral detachment.

The economy of the new society also requires to be clearly defined. It will be planned with the purpose of promoting the freedom and well-being of the individual. It will, on the one hand, eliminate production for profit and, on the other hand, avoid unnecessary concentration of control. It will not allow individual freedom to be jeopardised by considerations of technical efficiency. As such, the economy will be neither capitalist nor socialist, but co-operative. It will consist of a network of consumers' and producers' co-operatives, and the economic activities of the society shall be conducted and co-ordinated by the people through these institutions. The co-operative economy shall take full advantage of modern science and technology and effect equitable distribution of social surplus through universal social utility services.

The political and economic programme of the

movement will always be determined by the requirements of the attainment of the basic value of freedom, actually enjoyed individually by the members of the community.

The culture of the new society will grow in an atmosphere of individual freedom and morality. The function of the State will not be to regulate scientific and artistic growth, but to create conditions which will provide maximum scope and incentive for all forms of creative endeavour.

The primary task of the movement will be to bring about a cultural renaissance by propagating the philosophy of New Humanism and through its application to political, economic and other social problems.

To consolidate the intellectual basis of the movement, Radicals will continue to submit their philosophy to constant research, examine it in the light of modern scientific knowledge and experience, and extend its application to all the social sciences. They will, at the same time, propagate the essentials of the philosophy amongst the people as a whole by showing its relevance to their pressing needs. They will make the people conscious of the urge for freedom, encourage their self-reliance and awaken in them the sense of individual dignity, inculcate the values of rationalism and secular morality, and spread the spirit of cosmopolitan Humanism. By showing the people the way to solve their daily problems by popular initiative, the Radicals will combat ignorance, fatalism, blind faith and the sense of individual helplessness, which are the basis of authoritarianism.

They will put all the social traditions and institutions to the test of the humanist outlook.

Having created an atmosphere of individual initiative and co-operative effort, the Radicals will work with the people to build up People's Committees as the primary constituents of the democratic State, and co-operatives as the primary units of the co-operative Commonwealth. With the spread of the democratic outlook, and as a result of the functioning of these primary democratic institutions, the people will be able to exercise an increasing control over the government. Radicals will promote this process by encouraging the People's Committees in each constituency to nominate men and women of intellectual and moral detachment for election to the legislature. This will lead to the promulgation of a genuinely democratic constitution and the establishment of a co-operative economy. With a discriminating, responsible and freedom-loving membership, the People's Committees shall grow into the sovereign local units of social and political organisation and a country-wide network of these Committees shall form the dynamic structure of the truly democratic State.

APPENDIX C

SCIENCE AND SOCIETY

Science and Society

Summary of the inaugural Address at the Summer Camp for Higher Studies under the auspices of the Indian Renaissance Institute, Dehradun, held at Mussoorie from May 25th to June 4th, 1949.

The problems confronting the contemporary world were discussed in our last year's camp. The discussion led to the conclusion that the crisis of our time called for a new social philosophy which allotted a high place to morality in public life. The disgust with politics, that is, an unscrupulous scramble for power, and disapproval of economic exploitation of the majority by a minority, are no longer confined to the parties of the Left. They are shared practically by all. Leaders of political parties, actually engaged in the struggle for power, sanctimoniously condemn power-politics. Parties enjoying the patronage of the upper classes proclaim their intention to establish a classless society. Businessmen, big and small, call themselves Socialists. One hears the cry for morality on all sides: it has become incumbent on public men to talk of moral values.

Yet, there is little sign of improvement. The law of the jungle, scramble for political power and lust for economic loot, reign supreme; no single country can plead not guilty to the charge without laying itself open to the graver charge of telling the untruth.

Nevertheless, the mere fact that the absence of moral scruples in public life is generally deplored, that lip loyalty is pledged to moral values, is significant. If, in practice, politicians cannot be true to their professions, that is not necessarily proof of dishonesty. They are caught in a vicious circle. Engaged in a game, one must play it according to the rules. The fault of moralising politicians is the failure to realise that, so long as power remains the object of political practice, it cannot be handicapped by irrelevant scruples, it must be guided by the dictum—the end justifies the means. Caught in the whirl, even the best of men are bound to be pulled down to the lowest depth, which may appear as the pinnacle of power.

The disconcerting experience of the contemporary world compels thoughtful people to re-examine the fundamental principles of social philosophies from which different political theories—of the Right and of the Left, conservative and liberal, reactionary and revolutionary—are deduced. The experience is that in practice there is little difference, because capture of power, irrespective of the diversity of means advocated for the purpose, is the common postulate of all political theories. Morality in public life, therefore, presupposes a political theory which would not make capture of power the precondition for any necessary social change; and the new political theory must be deduced from a social philosophy which restores man in the place of primacy and sovereignty.

Morality being the dictate of conscience, it can be

practised only by individuals. Without moral men, there can be no moral society. Until now, all the architects and engineers of new social orders have reversed the order: they all postulated an ideal order as the condition for the free growth of human personalities. The Liberals believed that the ideal of a good life could be attained by good laws. As against their "reformism", Socialists and later on Communists maintained that economic reconstruction on the basis of common ownership was the condition for human development. The result has been eclipse of the individual by collectivities; totalitarianism and dictatorship in political practice have been the corollary to collectivisit social philosophies.

It is easy enough to place the individual in the centre of a social philosophy. As a matter of fact, individualism was the cardinal principle of the liberal social philosophy and political theory; and Liberalism was the source of inspiration for the magnificent achievements of modern civilisation. But in practice, the principle of individualism was reduced to an abstract doctrine; the sovereign individual to a legal fiction. The decay of Liberalism encouraged the rise of various collectivist doctrines which denied the possibility of individual freedom, ridiculed the idea as an empty abstraction, and proclaimed that, in order to be free, the individual must merge himself in the masses; in other words, find freedom in self-annihilation. If Liberalism had made a legal fiction of the sovereign individual, the socialist and communist conception of freedom is a fraud.

The cause of the decline of the liberal social philosophy was the ambiguity about the sanction of morality. It started with the excellent principle that the individual was a moral entity and, as such, sovereign. That is an ancient belief; in Europe, Christianity popularised it: man is a moral entity because he possesses the soul, which is a spark of the divine light of the universal moral order. In the beginning, that was an elevating idea; inspired by it, European humanity threw off the thraldom of the patriarchal and communal organisation of the mediaeval social order. But the religious faith in man's moral essence limits his sovereignty; indeed, it is a negation of the liberating concept. In the last analysis, it implies that man as man cannot be moral; to be so, he must feel himself subordinated to a superhuman power. With this paralysing sense of spiritual subservience, man can never be really free. Man's struggle against the doctrine of the necessity of his eternal spiritual subservience was the outstanding feature of the earlier stages of modern civilisation. Liberalism was born out of that struggle, which reached the high-water mark in the eighteenth century. The Enlightenment represented its afflorescence.

The shock of the French Revolution frightened Liberalism out of its wits. Natural religion was opposed to a transcendental moral order. As against the transcendentalism of the early nineteenth century moral philosophy, liberal social reformers and political theorists advanced the utility principle of morality. If in the former, ethical values were metaphysical concepts beyond the test of human experience, the latter deprived them of any objective standard, and that amounted to a negation of morality. Between the two, the civilised world was thrown into a moral confusion.

At the same time, the practice of parliamentary democracy and *laisser-faire* economics reduced the individual to a helpless position. The cumulative effect of moral confusion and social atomisation destroyed man's faith in himself. The collectivist ridicule of the idea of individual freedom corresponded with the experience of the bulk of the community. Having lost faith in himself, the individual welcomed the hope, offered by collectivist social philosophy, of finding security in the power of the masses. The human factor disappeared from politics. To sway the masses by appealing to base instincts and evil passions came to be the essence of political practice.

It is clear that moral philosophy itself must be placed on a sound basis before it can have a wholesome influence on social doctrines and political practice. The crucial question, therefore, is: What is the foundation of ethics? Can man be moral by himself? Until now, the prevailing opinion has been that man can behave morally only under compulsion, either supernatural or social. This view about the source of morality nullified the time-honoured belief that man is a moral entity; but that belief must be resurrected, and freed from its original limitation, if a really revolutionary social philosophy is to prescribe a rational political theory and a moral political practice.

A great advance in this direction was made during

the earlier centuries of the history of modern civilisation, when its pioneers made certain secular postulates about the nature of man and his place in nature. Their bold speculative thought, progressively reinforced by the expanding knowledge of nature, culminated in the scientific naturalism of the eighteenth century. The approach was humanist, which discarded the dogma of special creation and traced the origin of man in physical nature. Growing out of the background of a law-governed Universe, man must be a rational being; as such, he established the original society as an instrument for the development of his personality. The revolutionary discoveries of biology in the nineteenth century bore out the speculative postulates and rational hypotheses of the earlier thinkers. But just at that time, the ambiguities and inadequacies of Liberalism set the civilised world adrift towards a moral confusion.

The confusion was more confounded at the turning of the century when new discoveries of the physical sciences seemed to render untenable the classical concepts of substance and causality, which were the corner-stones of scientific naturalism. A neo-mysticism, claiming the authority of science, challenged the pretentions of Humanism. Not only the objective validity, but even the reality of human knowledge was disputed. Exaggerated emphasis on epistemology confused cosmological and ontological thought. An intellectual crisis aggravated the moral crisis.

Psychology preached irrationalism on the authority of science: in the garb of vague concepts of intuition, mysticism and transcendentalism returned to ethics. Man is irrational; he is instinctively moved by the blind urge of dark forces; therefore, the sanction of morality, either in private or public life, is the penal code and the police, or the priest. Except under the surveillance of these temporal and spiritual custodians of law and order, the law of the jungle would reign. The irony of our time is that the dreaded law of the jungle reigns supreme, nonetheless.

The only way out of this vicious circle is indicated by a moral philosophy which finds the sanction of its values in the rationality of the human being. But what is the sanction of the rationality of man? What is Reason? Is it again a metaphysical category, or a biological property? In the former case, the problem of the sanction of morality is not solved by tracing it in rationality. That is only referring one problem to another. As an expression of the reason in nature, rationality can be regarded as a biological function, and physical determinism is the Reason in nature. Otherwise, the classical concepts of natural law and moral order are meaningless. Modern sciences, physical as well as biological, put a content of objective truth in those concepts, which were originally hypothetical.

The object of these brief introductory remarks is to make it clear that the subjects to be discussed in this Camp have a direct bearing upon the practical problems of the contemporary world. The crying need of the time is to harmonise ethics with a social philosophy and political practice. The sovereignty of man, which must be the foundation of any revolutionary social philosophy, can be deduced only from the fact that man is a moral entity. It has been a time-honoured belief, which could not be sustained in practice; now the belief must be replaced by the knowledge of a fact: that man is moral because he is rational. The Universe is a moral order governed by laws inherent in itself. Man grows out of that backround.

Ethics must be the foundation of the moral philosophy which is the crying need of our time. In order to avoid the quicksand of transcendentalism and the pitfalls of relativity, ethics must be integrated in a general philosophy. We do not want to build yet another castle in the air which will not stand the test of the next storm. A humanist ethics based on a naturalist rationalism can be built only on the rock-bottom of a mechanistic cosmology and physical-realist ontology. Therefore, we must begin our discussion by examining the problems raised by modern physics. The next step is to find the connecting link between the world of dead matter and living nature. It is no longer a missing link; it solves the problem of the origin of life. If we discover that life originates in course of the mechanistic process of nature, human rationality can be deduced from the background of the law-governed physical Universe: the imaginary gulf between physics and psychology is thus bridged and the most baffiling problems of philosophy, the epistemological problems, are solved. Truth ceases to be a metaphysical concept: it stands out as the content of knowledge. In the light of the basic nature of truth, the nature of other value 's more clearly visible, and they can be rationally arranged in a proper hierarchy. Having thus obtained our moral values in the world in which man has his being and becoming, we shall be able to harmonise them with a social philosophy which indicates the humanist approach to the economic and political problems confronting the contemporary world.

APPENDIX D

THE FOUNDATION OF A NEW SOCIAL PHILOSOPHY

The Foundation of a New Social Philosophy

Speech at the First All-India Convention of Radical Humanists, Calcutta, February 4th, 1951, in the open session presenting the statements on political and economic problem:

The two statements submitted here for public consideration outline ideas which most probably have been expounded by others also. No patent is claimed for them. But they certainly have not as yet been put to practice anywhere. This fact, however, does not mean any adverse reflexion on those who may have held and preached those ideas previously. The failure to practise them has been due to a wrong notion of human nature. which vitiated social philosophy from time immemorial. Economic and political practice are forms of social relations, and these. in the last analysis, are relations between individuals. The individual human being is the basic category of social science. including political theories and economic doctrines. Therefore, a correct idea about human nature must be the point of departure of a social practice which may show a way out of the present atmosphere of frustration and helplessness.

The previous speakers have mentioned that these statements suggesting a new approach to the most burning problems confornting our country. have been deduced from a comprehensive general philosophy of life. The fundamental principle of that philosophy is a clearly defined idea about the nature of man. This again is nothing altogether new; ever since the seventeenth century, when the attempt to develop a comprehensive social philosophy began, all pioneers of the movement started from some hypothesis about the nature of man. There were two assumptions with many variations: Firstly, the general idea was that man is either selfish by nature and is instinctively concerned only with his own interest. Secondly, human nature is to believe in some benevolent supernatural power. Though it appeared to be the antithesis of the former, the latter assumption was historically associated with the earlier Christian belief in man's original sin. So it amounted to that man was sinful (bad) by nature, but could be good by virtue of his readiness to subordinate himself to a heavenly father or metaphysical power.

With one or the other ot tnese basic assumptions, no social philosophy could conceive of society except as a coercive organisation, to be ruled either by man-made laws or providential ordinance; both meant to curb the evil instincts of man. In ethier case, society was to be a prison—penal or reformatory. In one, man must surrender his birthright of freedom to the sovereignty of the State; in the other, he must believe that life on this earth is dominated and dictated by some providential will or superhuman forces which he can never comprehend. In either case, man is helpless, and can have no freedom in social relations, and no initiative in political and economic practice.

With these prevailing views of human nature, it was not possible to develop such a social philosophy which allowed deduction of economic theories and political doctrines to guarantee freedom and equality in practice. The result is the present crisis of modern civilisation. Everybody talks about the crisis of our time; books have been written about it. Practically all the outstanding intellectuals of our time are trying to understand its nature and lay bare its causes. But all these well-meaning and often competent attempts are stultified by the absence of an integral view of the crisis. Some say it is an economic crisis. All of them do not believe in economic determinism. But the view that man is selfish by nature and that the incentive of all economic activities is personal gain, logically leads to that belief. Karl Marx raised the economic interpretation of history on the level of a social philosophy. Some of the contemporary philosophers pretend to be wiser than Karl Marx and criticise his interpretation of history. But their point of departure is the same as that of Marx. Modern liberal sociology has not discarded the doctrine of the economic man. If man is primarily an economic being, then material gain is the determining factor of social development.

Given this point of departure, the crisis of the modern world must be regarded as essentially economic. It then follows that an economic reconstruction of society, replacement of the outmoded capitalist system by a new order, will end the crisis. Attempts have been made and are being made to develop a social philosophy on this line; and they are not confined only to those who advocate a revolutionary reconstruction of society. More cautious and conservative economic thinkers are also making similar attempts. There are few who do not see the need for a revision of economic theories and readjustment of economic practice accordingly. Those who oppose revolutionary reconstruction suggest the so-called mixed economy as the cure of the crisis of the modern time. One of the previous speakers has pointed out the implications of mixed economy, and how dangerous they are.

The socialist or communist plans of economic reconstruction attract greater attention and have motivated powerful popular movements. More than thirty years ago, the revolution took place in one country, which began economic reconstruction according to communist doctrines and plans. A number of other countries fell in line subsequently. Of late, they have been joined by the largest Asian country. Consequently, we are now in a position to judge if revolutionary reconstruction of economy brings about an all-round improvement. Even the measure of economic equality under communism is deceptive and doubtful. A considerable increase in industrial and agricultural production has indeed taken place in Russia. The default of the newer Communist States in this respect may be explained by the shortness of the experiment. But in the Fatherland of Socialism itself, consumption has not kept pace with increased production. That means that the new economic system has not contributed even to the material welfare of the common people. But granted that some advance has been made in that direction, and that it is a good beginning, one cannot ignore the price of this doubtful blessing. The price is forfeiture of political and intellectual freedom, and cultural regimentation. This experience exposes the fallacy of social philosophy based on the doctrine of the economic man.

The exorbitant price for problematical economic security and doubtful material welfare has to be paid whenever the government of a country, whether dictatorial or formally democratic, claims to be the guardian of the welfare of the people and the latter expected the government to do everything for them. In such a situation, a government is entitled to demand the power to do things in its own way. Political dictatorship, either *de facto* or *de jure*, denial of freedom, intellectual regimentation,' logically follow from the tradition that people by themselves cannot do anything. Consequently, society is divided into the people and the rulers. Whether the latter are feudal, bourgeois or proletarian, the distinction necessarily leads to the eclipse of liberty.

There are people who say that they do not believe in economic determinism. They also advocate replacement of capitalism by a more equitable, classless, economic order, but reject the dictatorial method of Communism. They offer the alternative of the so-called democratic Socialism, or the Welfare State. This experiment is being made in Britain. The distinction between the economic theories of capitalism and Socialism is getting lost in practice. Because both start from the doctrine of the economic man. The idea of a Welfare State was conceived by bourgeois Liberalism in the age of capitalist prosperity towards the end of the nineteenth century. The proletarian Labour Party has taken over an idea of the bourgeoisie. Its practice is called democratic Socialism. It is democratic because under it the people can vote freely. But what are its economic blessings? The Welfare State undertakes to provide every wage-earner with a set of false teeth free of cost; that presumably is his birthright. But he may not get meat more than the size of a matchbox for the whole week. There is something fraudulent in this welfare. Money is taken out of one pocket of the worker and put into his other pocket in the form of benefits; in the process the money loses about 20-25% of its value. These are facts and not theories. Even under democratic Socialism, economic welfare must be purchased; the price is forfeiture of individual liberty and regimentation. The practice of any theory, conservative, liberal, revolutionary, which starts from the doctrine of the economic man, must lead to the loss of freedom and the degradation of man. If man is selfish and irrational by nature, society must be a coercive organisation, prison house to be guarded by earthly policemen backed up by heavenly colleagues. Economic determinism therefore cannot be the social philosophy which is required to lead civilised mankind out of the present crisis.

Others diagnose the disease as a crisis of political theories and institutions. They recommend that the parliamentary system should be improved by various ingenious devices. It is hardly necessary to go into an examination of the mechanical remedies suggested; they are bound to fail as long as greater importance is attached to institutions than to men. The central fallacy of these political theories is to place institutions above men, to ignore that institutions are created by men. Any attempt at social reconstruction to promote economic welfare and political liberty must begin with man. If men are selfish by nature, and therefore predisposed to authoritarianism, the best of theories and constitutions cannot build institutions which would guarantee freedom and promote general welfare. It is quite obvious that such institutions can only be created by men, who may not as yet be free, but who want to be free.

The statement of a new approach to the problems of economic and political reconstruction is deduced from a social philosophy which resulted from an enquiry into the cause of the crisis of modern civilisation. The enquiry was undertaken on the basis of the experience of the political movement in this country and also the lessons of the contemporary history of the world. It led to the discovery that all the evils of our time—political instability, economic insecurity, impoverishment of the masses, rise of totalitarianism, danger of dictatorship, the growing menace of yet another world war, to mention only the most outstanding ones could be traced to one single cause, namely, wrong notions about human nature. Social philosophies built on the different variations of the wrong notion ultimately undermined man's faith in himself. The crisis of modern civilisation, in the last analysis, therefore, is a spiritual crisis.

Others also reached the same conclusion, but believed

that the conflict in the mind of man, his moral disintegration, was the cumulative result of his social experience. The corollary to this conclusion is that a reconstruction of human society on the basis of more democratic political institutions and more equitable economic relations is the crying need of our time.

But practice demonstrated the superficiality of this view; the disease defied the remedy prescribed. Political instability spread even to the few remaining countries which still retained the facade of parliamentary democracy, the ominous shadow of totalitarianism (nationalist, socialist, communist) eclipsed liberty; the appeal of dictatorship grew more and more irresistible. The economic crisis aggravated everywhere; attempts to provide economic security spelled drift towards regimentation, even under formal parliamentary democracy; violent revolutions destroyed liberty, while the utopia of social justice and economic equality remained as far as ever.

The disconcerting experience demanded a more penetrating enquiry, which led to the discovery that the roots of all the evils of the modern world could be traced to the absence of man's faith in himself. If better institutions are the need of the time, there must be men with the faith in the capacity to do so The new institutions, to be stable, must be built from the bottom up. That cannot be done by governments, political parties, even great dictators. Institutions imposed from above collapse when they are not sustained by the intelligent will of individual men and women composing society. But today men live in an atmosphere of helplessness and frustration. In this atmosphere, nothing whatsoever can be built. That is why the imposing structure of modern civilisation is crumbling.

That is a tragedy; but there is greater tragedy. Men have lost their faith in God also. Today, in despair, they do not seek solace in traditional religion. The spiritual crisis of our age expresses itself in the rise of a new religion; the masses are the God of the vulgar and secular religion; the political party is the new priesthood, the leader is the high-priest. They have no faith in individuals, but they believe that, when thousands and thousands of helpless individuals come together, to follow the party and the leader, an irresistible power generates. It is a blind faith, so very blind as not to notice the curious arithmetic: a zero is nothing, but when millions of zero are put together, the total becomes the almighty God. This new God is worshipped as the Masses, the Nation, or a class; and entire continents are thus deified, for example, the mystic cult of the resurgence of Asia.

The remedy is suggested by the diagnosis of the disease. We shall have to strike at the root of the evil. The new social philosophy must start from an idea about human nature which will revive the hope of man having faith in himself. If it is true that man by nature is a believer in some power greater than himself, and therefore cannot think of doing anything by himself, then the cherished idea of human freedom must be abandoned. The religious man cannot think of improving God's creation. On the other hand, the assumption that human nature is selfish logically leads to the view that society can never do without political coercion of the State or moral dictation of religion. So, this alternative view of human nature also rules out the possibility of freedom.

The history of civilisation, however, proves that both the assumptions about human nature were equally unfounded. Throughout history, heretics were the pioneers of human progress. Faith is based on ignorance; if it was the foundation of human nature, knowledge would not be possible, and man would be still living in blissful ignorance. As regards the other assumption, it is true that his own existence is the primary concern of man; but it is equally true that his selfishness breeds the capacity to outgrow it. The theory of class struggle ignores the fact that co-operation has always been a stronger social factor. Otherwise, society would have fallen to pieces at the dawn of civilisation. History, therefore, warrants the view that neither is human nature incorrigibly selfish, nor is it founded on the faith in the super-human. Modern science corroborates this view, which can inspire a social philosophy capable of showing a way out of the crisis of our time.

In the past, inadequate knowledge kept human nature shrouded in mystery. Today there is little reason to call man, "the unknown." Nor is there any ground for the venerable faith in his divine essence. As a biological form, man is a physical entity. The entire process from the fertilisation of an ovum to the birth of the full-grown child, is a physical phenomenon. No extraneous element enters in the process at any point. Whatever, distinguishes the human being from the lower animals, the so-called soul, is not a divine spark. Nowhere could the divine spark smuggle itself into the physical process. What is called soul is but the sum total of the diverse manifestations of life, which itself is a physico-chemical phenomenon. Therefore we rule out the doctrine that. man being differentiated from animals by the possession of a divine spark, to believe in the transcendental source of his humanness is the foundation of his nature. Thus liberated from the venerable prejudice of his spiritual origin, which persuades him to accept spiritual slavery as the token of his superiority, man can think of being free as man. The spiritual liberation will give him the confidence in the capacity to participate voluntarily in the collective human endeavour to build a free society Anthropology also helps us in the enquiry into human nature. It proves that human society did not originate in an ad hoc control. Primitive man had to struggle against his environments. He could do so more successfully in co-operation with others. The instinct of self-preservation and struggle for existence led to the foundation of civil society. Instinct is primitive reason. Man therefore is essentially a rational being. Modern knowledge of biology also allows this deduction. Rudiments of reason, the ability to connect experiences, can be traced in lower animals. Rationality, therefore, is a biological function which can very highly develop in the highest biological form. Rationality can subordinate man's selfishness to enlightened self-interest, which is a social virtue.

Now we can discard another idea which has bedevilled modern social thought; the idea of conflict and competition. Some economists say that competition is the lever of all progress; and revolutionaries attach the same significance to social conflict which they call class struggle. No doubt there have been conflicts, and there will be. But an unprejudiced study of history reveals that the desire to be helpful to fellow-men is a more fundamental human trait than competition and conflict. However, religion and social philosophies based on it and other wrong assumptions made man forget his innate rationality. Religion having done havoc in the past, philosophy in our time reached the cult of irrationalism. At the same time, the experience of conflict discouraged the spirit of co-operation. The cumulative result is man's loss of faith in himself.

The scientific knowledge about human nature reveals the root of the cultural crisis of our times, and should enable us to discover an entirely new approach to the baffling problems of modern life. The crisis does not affect just this or that aspect of social existence; it envelops the whole being of man. Therefore it can be called a spiritual crisis, a crisis of the soul of man. Man has forgotten what he is. The only way out of the impasse is to help him remember that he is a man, and not a slave either of a divine slave-driver or of any terrestial power.

The fundamental principles of this new philosophy of life were outlined three years ago. We called it New or Scientific or Integral Humanism. There is nothing altogether new in it. Humanism is as old as history. The common feature of Humanism throughout the ages has been the belief that there are certain human values which transcend all other considerations, and to develop the human personality is the main purpose of life; political practice and social institutions, economic organisations, educational endeavours, should all serve the basic purpose of life. But in the olden times the wrong idea of human nature contradicted the humanist philosophy of life. Therefore, classical Humanism failed to hold its own against the opposing views of life, which harmonised with the wrong notions about human nature. But to-day scientific knowledge as well as a careful reading of history enable Humanism to challenge the wrong notions about human nature and thus free itself from all contradictions and fallacies. Therefore, we call it New Humanism. Since its newness is derived from modern scientific knowledge, the more appropriate name is scientific Humanism. We restate the principle of the sovereignty and primacy of man not as a dogma, but with the support of scientific knowledg

That is the point of departure of a new approach to the various problems of modern life. Take for instance the economic problems of our country. Everybody knows that things are going from bad to worse. And the easiest thing to do is to blame somebody for this state of affairs, and the government is the obvious scapegoat. All complaints against prevailing conditions amount to abusing the present government, which is followed up by the demand for an alternative government under the control of the complainant. It is maintained that such a change of government will solve all problems; but the pretenders to power do not explain how. If they really knew how to solve the problems, why don't they let the established government have the benefit of their wisdom? There is no reason to believe that the men in power are less concerned with popular welfare than those who aspire to replace them. Governments may be mistaken and not do the right thing. But after all, they are also composed of human beings, capable of moral judgment. Therefore, if you appeal to their good sense and point out repeatedly that they can do things better, they may listen to you. But if you insist that they must get out so that you may be in power, their back will be up, and they will insist on pursuing their mistaken policy. The men in power are handicapped by the anxiety to remain in power. That desire on their part is morally no more reprehensible than the desire of others to replace them. Potentially, one man is as good as the other. To appeal to the rationality and the moral sense of the men in power therefore, is the only manner of purifying politics. This is not an abstract moralist attitude. It is the most practical approach to the problem of political practice. The politicians in power must have votes in the next elections. They must therefore listen to public opinion if it advocates a more promising approach to problems which have baffled them.

There are two lines of approach. One is fundamental. You cannot cure things by imposing reforms from above. It must be done from the bottom. So long as the people want their problems to be solved for them, they must be prepared to obey, to follow blindly, to be regimented. On the contrary, if they want freedom, they must prove that they are capable of being free. They can do that by declaring that as human beings they can do whatever they expect others to do for them. They may not be able to rebuild the whole of Indian economy. But they can indicate the way. It is the formation of local co-operative organisations as the nuclei of a new system of economy. There is no reason why the government should not encourage popular initiative. Without doubting the sincerity of its professions and intentions, we must persevere in appealing to its good sense, while doing things on our own initiative.

They say that economic prosperity of India is conditional on her ability to build up heavy industries. But they also say that the condition cannot be created with India's own resources. She requires foreign aid. But dollars are not coming. What are we to do? Can we do without them? We can. To point out how, is the purpose of our statement on a new approach to the problems of economic reconstruction.

Consistently with the belief, based on the knowledge that man is essentially rational, we appeal to the government with the hope that it may change its policy. At the same time, we say that popular initiative is not precluded by whatever the government may or may not do.

Humanist approach to the problem of democracy

in India is equally rational and realistic. It advocates initiative from below. Formal democracy has not been a blessing. It is bound to be less so when the electorate is politically illiterate, as in India. Party politics will not establish political freedom. It confounds democracy with demagogy. Those who are dissatisfied with the present government, propose to organise an opposition party with the object of capturing power. Under the parliamentary system, power is to be captured through the ballot box. In order to win the election, the opposition party must promise to do what the present government has failed to do. It does not explain how it will make the miracle. The present government may not be composed of angels and supermen, nor will the alternative one be. There are objective difficulties, which will baffle the one as they have done the other. But party politics does not make room for such honest admission. It must promise miracles, belief in which presupposes irrationalism on the part of the electorate. Election propaganda, therefore, appeals to emotion and blind faith. Only consummate demagogues can succeed in it. Measured by this standard of formal democracy—the method of counting heads—the avowed dictator Hitler was the most successful democrat of our time. By inflaming the passions of the people demagogically, he obtained their almost unanimous support several times. The voice of the people ceases to be the voice of God when the people ceases to be an aggregate of men capable of moral and rational judgment. The demagogic practice of formal democracy may degrade the sovereign people to the status of a mass of voting robots. In India such degradation of formal democracy is practically predetermined by the cultural predisposition of the people to believe blindly and to except miracles.

Intelligent people would take to this risky path with their eyes open for the reason that the only alternative is Communism. On the other hand, the none too reassuring experience of parliamentary democracy in other countries induces wooly-headed idealists to flirt with Communism. It is argued that Russian Communism is bad, but in China Communism has taken the democratic path. There, Communism is supposed to have triumphed with the support of the people. This idea of Communism being purified by nationalism is simply not true. In China also it means violence, suppression of all liberty and all the rest of the familiar story. Whether it be of the Russian or Chinese variety, Communism will bring in its wake a long period of terror, regimentation, suppression of liberty, most probably civil war and chaos. It is sheer madness to welcome that catastrophe with the hope that the golden utopia may be waiting on the other side of the uncharted sea of blood and tears.

Is there no third alternative? Must we fall back upon the intellectual lethargy of choosing the lesser evil? And even that judgment will create endless confusion, because it will be a matter of opinion and predisposition. While rejecting Communism, we cannot ignore the defects of formal democracy. It will not establish political freedom in this country, where the cultural preconditions for democratic practice are absent. In this atmosphere, formal democracy will not only easily degenerate into vulgar demagogy and deception; it may indeed prepare the way to a dictatorship with popular support. On the other hand, beginning from scratch, we in India need not be handicapped by the tradition of formalism. We can give democracy a chance by laying down its human foundation. The coming election gives us the opportunity to do so. We should advise the people not to take any party on its words, and help them to examine critically the promises made during the election campaign. All the promises may be sincerely made; but they may be unrealistic and therefore meant to deceive the people. The danger of democracy degenerating into demagogy can be headed off only by helping the people to develop their capacity of judgment. And only a social philosophy which holds that man is essentially rational can inspire us to undertake the task of building a democratic order on the solid foundation of an intelligent electorate, which will not be swayed by appeals to emotion.

This endeavour to lay down the humanist foundation of a democratic order must be coordinated with the cooperative reconstruction of the economic life. The result will be creation of a chain of local republics in which democracy will be real, because it will be direct, and economic problems solved on the basis of local resources, with the intelligent initiative and cooperative effort of the citizens Whoever are more concerned with the freedom and welfare of the people than with power to rule in the name of the people, can begin doing things by themselves, irrespective of the attitude of the established government. But they must have confidence in themselves, and the confidence is given by the humanist philosophy of life.

The practical details of what should be done and how—are outlined in the two statements submitted for public consideration. They do not claim any finality. They do not lay down the blueprint of the future. They only indicate a new approach to problems which have baffled the politicians. Agreement with it will not mean any organisational commitment, involve no party discipline. Our appeal is to reason and moral responsibility. The response to this entirely disinterested appeal will be the measure of hope for the future not only of our country, but of the modern civilisation.